TEMPTING
CHEESECAKES

TEMPTING CHEESECAKES

Barbara Maher

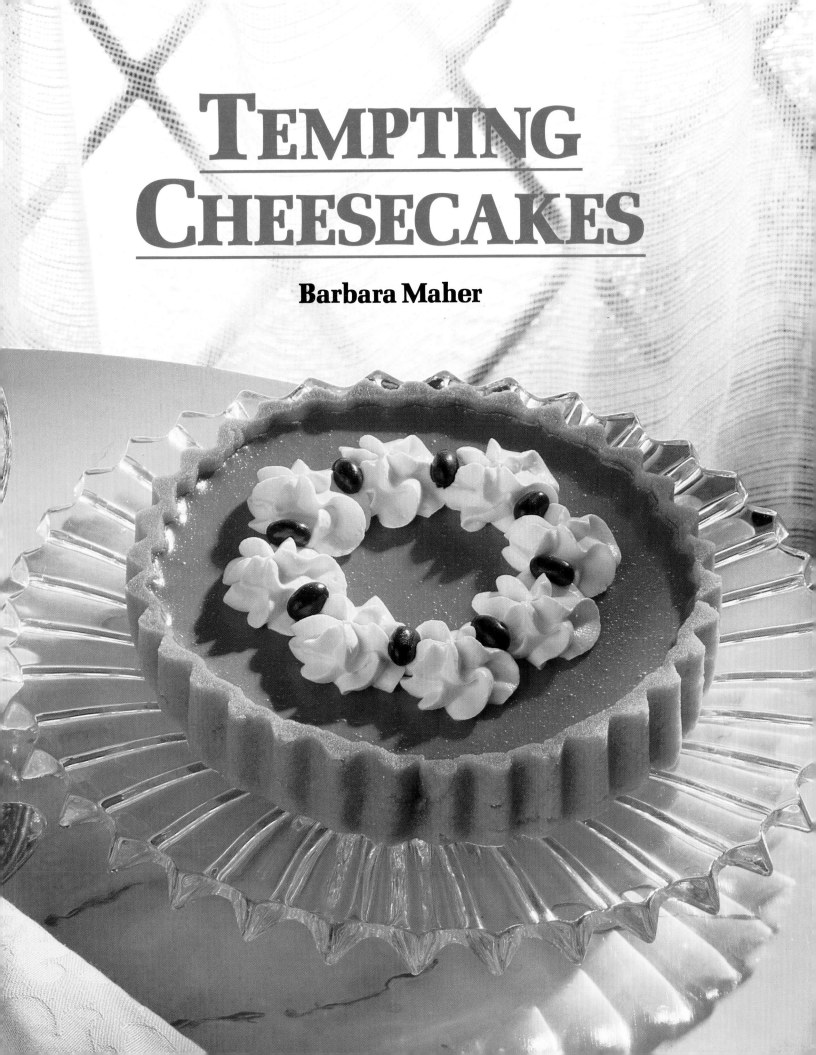

CONTENTS

First published in 1985 by Octopus Books Ltd
59 Grosvenor Street, London W1

© 1985 Hennerwood Publications Ltd

ISBN 0 86273 135 6

Produced by Mandarin Publishers Ltd
22a Westlands Road
Quarry Bay, Hong Kong

Printed in Hong Kong

INTRODUCTION

Although cheesecakes have been eaten in the Middle East for centuries, it is only in recent times that they have become a popular part of the British diet. The early cheesecakes were always cooked, and usually consisted of a pastry base or wrapping which contained a filling of soft cheese enriched with eggs, sugar or honey and enhanced with spices or aromatic flavourings. This tradition has been maintained and encouraged ever since by European cooks, who have introduced new ingredients such as fresh and candied fruits, nuts and liqueurs.

Uncooked cheesecakes from the United States are a comparatively recent introduction. They are quite different to cooked cheesecakes, having, in most cases, a crunchy biscuit crumb base, and a creamy gelatine-set filling. They are usually very rich and are especially good served as luxury after-dinner desserts.

Here is a world-wide selection of cheesecake recipes with ideas from Austria, Hungary, France, Russia, Germany and Switzerland as well as from the USA and the Middle East. Some will be familiar – every collection of cheesecakes has to include the classic recipes – others will be less well known, and hopefully delicious surprises.

A cooked cheesecake should appear well risen and golden coloured and should be shrinking away slightly from the edges of the tin. Test by inserting a skewer or wooden toothpick gently into the centre of the cake, which is always the slowest part to cook, and remove it carefully. It should come out clean and dry; if any mixture adheres, bake the cake for a few minutes longer. Baked cheesecakes have a tendency to collapse and crack as they cool. This does not affect the texture or flavour, but simply adds to their appeal.

Conventional, fan-assisted and fan ovens
The baking temperatures and times given in this book are intended for conventional ovens. Many new electric ovens are now fitted with a fan to assist the circulation of heat. Because of this constant and even temperature cakes are inclined to bake far more quickly and have a tendency to become too dry. As a general rule it is necessary to reduce the oven temperature by between 20° and 25°C in every 100°C to correct this, but for the best results it is important to consult the accompanying literature for your particular oven for precise information.

HINTS AND BASIC RECIPES

Types of Cheese

Most of the cheesecakes in this book are made with curd cheese which has a butterfat content of about 12%. The flavour is good, but not too rich to mask the other ingredients, and the texture is dry. If you have difficulty obtaining it, use equal quantities of cream cheese and cottage cheese mixed, but take care to drain both of them well before using.

Ricotta cheese, the Italian equivalent of cottage cheese, also contains very little fat but has a smooth texture and mild, sweet flavour. It is well worth trying, but be sure when you buy it that it is very fresh as it spoils quickly.

Beating Egg Whites

Always beat whites in a spotlessly clean large bowl. For best results use a wire whisk or hand-held electric beater. Do not interrupt the beating or the egg whites will collapse and become watery. Start by beating slowly, then as the whites froth up increase the speed, lifting the beater through and round the mixture whilst rotating the bowl, so as to incorporate as much air as possible. Beaten egg whites should be cream-coloured, well expanded and stand in firm, well-formed peaks. You should be able to turn the bowl over without the mixture sliding out. Overbeaten egg whites look granular and slightly lumpy, then quickly start to separate and turn to water. At this stage they are unusable. Egg whites that are to be folded into a soft, runny mixture should not be beaten for quite as long.

Folding in Beaten Egg Whites

Beaten egg whites must be folded into a mixture as soon as they are prepared, with a large metal spoon. Drop one third of the egg white on to the mixture and lightly and quickly cut down through the mixture with a figure of eight motion, turning the bowl as you work. Repeat with the other two portions of egg white. Do not stir as this will break down the egg white and produce a heavy and wet cake. Once the egg white has been added bake the cake immediately, otherwise the mixture will collapse.

BISCUIT OR BREADCRUMB BASE

Makes one 20 cm (8 inch) base
100 g (4 oz) digestive biscuits, crushed, or fresh
  breadcrumbs, toasted
50 g (2 oz) caster sugar
½ teaspoon ground cinnamon
½ teaspoon ground nutmeg
50 g (2 oz) butter
1 tablespoon apricot jam

Makes one 22 or 24 cm (8½ or 9½ inch) base
150 g (5 oz) digestive biscuits, crushed, or fresh
  breadcrumbs, toasted
75 g (3 oz) caster sugar
½ teaspoon ground cinnamon
½ teaspoon ground nutmeg
75 g (3 oz) butter
1½ tablespoons apricot jam

Makes one 26 or 28 cm (10½ or 11 inch) base
175g (6 oz) digestive biscuits, crushed, or fresh
  breadcrumbs, toasted
100 g (4 oz) caster sugar
1 teaspoon ground cinnamon
1 teaspoon ground nutmeg
100 g (4 oz) butter
2 tablespoons apricot jam

Preparation time: 10 minutes plus chilling
Cooking time: 5 minutes

1. Line the base of the chosen tin with non-stick silicone paper and grease the sides well.
2. Mix the breadcrumbs or biscuit crumbs with the sugar and spices.
3. Gently melt the butter and apricot jam in a large pan, then remove from the heat, stir in the crumb mixture and combine well.
4. Press evenly and firmly into the prepared tin using the back of a spoon.
5. Leave to chill whilst the filling is prepared.

Variation:
For a Chocolate biscuitcrumb base use dark chocolate digestives rather than plain ones and reduce the sugar quantity as follows: 1 tablespoon for an 18-20 cm (7-8 inch) base, 1½ tablespoons for a 22-24 cm (8½-9½ inch) base, 2 tablespoons for a 26-30 cm (10½-12 inch) base.

NUT AND BREADCRUMB BASE

Makes one 20 cm (8 inch) base
75 g (3 oz) toasted breadcrumbs
40 g (1½ oz) grated or ground nuts
40 g (1½ oz) vanilla or caster sugar
½ teaspoon butter, melted
1 tablespoon apricot jam

Makes one 22 or 24 cm (8½ or 9½ inch) base
100 g (4 oz) toasted breadcrumbs
50 g (2 oz) grated or ground nuts
50 g (2 oz) vanilla or caster sugar
¾ teaspoon ground cinnamon
50 g (2 oz) butter, melted
1½ tablespoons apricot jam

Makes one 26 or 28 cm (10½ or 11 inch) base
150 g (5 oz) toasted breadcrumbs
65 g (2½ oz) vanilla or caster sugar
1 heaped teaspoon ground cinnamon
75 g (3 oz) butter, melted
2 tablespoons apricot jam

Preparation time: 15 minutes plus chilling
Cooking time: 5 minutes

This is a very adaptable cheesecake base. Use grated walnuts, grated toasted hazelnuts, or grated pecans or ground almonds, according to the individual recipe.

1. Line the base of the tin with non-stick silicone paper and grease the sides well.
2. Mix together the breadcrumbs, grated or ground nuts, sugar and cinnamon.
3. In a large pan, gently melt the butter with the apricot jam. Remove from the heat, stir in the crumb mixture and combine well.
4. Press firmly into the tin with the back of a spoon.
5. Leave to chill whilst the filling is prepared.

Vanilla Sugar
A jar of vanilla-perfumed sugar is always useful in the kitchen and can be used to give a subtle and authentic vanilla flavour that is far superior to synthetic vanilla essence. Fill an airtight jar with caster sugar and plunge a vanilla pod into it. Store in a cool place, away from the light. One pod will perfume 1 kg (2 lb) of sugar, and will keep its flavour for about a year. As the sugar is used up, simply top up the level in the jar with fresh sugar. Use instead of plain caster sugar in any recipe where a vanilla flavour is required, remembering to omit any vanilla essence that is included in the recipe.

SHORTCRUST PASTRY

Makes one 20 or 22 cm (8 or 8½ inch) pastry case or 12 tartlet shells:
120 g (4½ oz) plain flour, sifted
pinch of salt
75 g (3 oz) butter, chilled and cut into cubes
1 tablespoon caster sugar (optional, see below)
1 egg yolk
up to 1½ tablespoons iced water

Preparation time: 15 minutes plus chilling
Cooking time: 25 minutes for a pastry case
               15 minutes for tartlet shells
Oven: 200°C, 400°F, Gas Mark 6
then: 180°C, 350°F, Gas Mark 4 (for pastry case)

This pastry is very elastic and can be rolled out easily. Allow it to rest for a few minutes after rolling, to let it spring back, before lining the tin(s). For Savoury shortcrust pastry proceed as below but omit the sugar.

1. Sift the flour and salt into a bowl and make a well in the centre. Add the cubed butter, then lightly and swiftly rub the mixture to a fine breadcrumb texture. Mix in the sugar.
2. Add the egg yolk and work the mixture into a soft, but not sticky dough, moistening as necessary with the iced water. Roll the dough into a ball.
3. With the heel of the hand, blend the pastry – a small amount at a time – by pushing it away from you on a floured worktop. When it is smooth and pliable gather it into a ball, dredge it with flour, wrap it in clingfilm or foil and chill for 30 minutes. Ⓐ
4. Roll out the pastry (see above) and line the tin or tartlet shells. If using a springform tin the pastry should cover the base and extend 2.5 cm (1 inch) up the sides. For a pastry case bake in a preheated oven for 10 minutes, then lower the temperature and bake for a further 15 minutes. For tartlet shells bake at higher temperature for 15 minutes. Fill when cooled. Ⓐ

Ⓐ The pastry can be prepared 3-4 days in advance. Wrap in clingfilm and chill until required.

> **Par-baking**
> This technique is normally used for pastry bases that do not have sides. Use the base of a spring-form tin as a mould. Grease it, line with pastry and prick all over with a fork. Cover with foil or greaseproof paper, weigh down with beans, and place on a hot baking sheet in an oven preheated to 200°C, 400°F, Gas Mark 6. Bake for 10-15 minutes until the pastry is set and lightly coloured. Cool on a wire tray.

SWEET SHORTCRUST PASTRY

Makes one 20 or 22 cm (8 or 8½ inch) pastry case or 10 tartlet shells:
120 g (4½ oz) plain flour, sifted
pinch of salt
3 tablespoons caster sugar
½ teaspoon grated lemon zest
1 egg yolk
90 g (3½ oz) butter, chilled and cut into cubes

Makes one 24 or 26 cm (9½ or 10½ inch) pastry case or 14 tartlet shells:
165 g (5½ oz) plain flour, sifted
pinch of salt
50 g (2 oz) caster sugar
1 small egg
100 g (4 oz) butter, chilled and cut into cubes

Preparation time: 15 minutes plus chilling
Cooking time: 25 minutes for a pastry case
               15 minutes for tartlet shells
Oven: 200°C, 400°F, Gas Mark 6
then: 180°C, 350°F, Gas Mark 4 (for pastry case)

This pastry must be well chilled before it is used as it is more crumbly than shortcrust pastry. If the pastry is difficult to roll out it may be pressed into the tins by hand, patching any small cracks with small pieces of pastry.

1. Prepare the pastry as for steps 1-3 of Shortcrust pastry, adding the lemon zest with the sugar.
2. Roll out the chilled pastry, line the tin or tartlet shells and bake as for Shortcrust pastry.

> **Baking blind**
> Pastry cases for cheesecakes usually need to be baked before the filling is put in to prevent them becoming soggy. Grease the tin and line the base and sides with pastry. Prick all over with a fork. Press a sheet of tin foil or greaseproof paper lightly into the base and up the sides of the tin and weigh it down with dried beans, rice or pastry pebbles (which can be used again and again for this purpose); these will prevent the pastry from rising during cooking. Place the tin on a hot baking sheet in an oven preheated to 200°C, 400°F, Gas Mark 6, and bake for 10 minutes, then reduce the oven temperature to 180°C, 350°F, Gas Mark 4 and bake for a further 15 minutes until pale golden. Remove the foil or paper and weights, brush lightly with beaten egg white and cook for a further 5 minutes. Cool on a wire tray in the tin.

YEAST DOUGH

Makes one 26 cm (10½ inch) pastry case
150 ml (¼ pint) milk, warmed to 80°F, 25°C
20 g (¾ oz) fresh yeast
65g (2½ oz) plus 1 teaspoon caster sugar
300 g (11 oz) strong plain flour, sifted
75 g (3 oz) butter
2 eggs
1 tablespoon grated lemon zest
pinch of salt

Preparation time: 40 minutes plus rising
Cooking time: 25-30 minutes
Oven: 190°C, 375°F, Gas Mark 5

If you prefer to use dried yeast rather than fresh, use a generous 10g (¼ oz) and follow the preparation instructions on the packet.

1. Pour the milk into a warmed bowl and crumble in the fresh yeast. Add the teaspoon of sugar and stir. Beat in 75 g (3 oz) of the flour, beat well then cover and leave to rise for 10-15 minutes until doubled in bulk.
2. Meanwhile beat together the butter and remaining sugar until light and fluffy. Beat in the eggs, one at a time, and the lemon zest.
3. Sift the remaining flour and salt into a bowl, make a well in the centre and pour in the butter and sugar mixture and the yeast mixture. Beat well, then knead hard until the dough is firm and elastic and rolls cleanly off the side of the bowl. Cover and leave to rise until doubled in bulk. This may take up to an hour.
4. Proceed according to recipe instructions.

Curd cheese and spinach filo parcels in preparation (recipe page 71)

FATLESS SPONGE CAKE

Makes one 24 or 26 cm (9½ or 10½ inch) cake
1 tablespoon flour mixed with 1 tablespoon sugar
120g (4½ oz) caster sugar
5 eggs, separated
1 tablespoon grated lemon zest
120 g (4½ oz) plain flour, well sifted

Preparation time: 20 minutes
Cooking time: 30 minutes
Oven: 180°C, 350°F, Gas Mark 4

1. Grease the tin and line the base with non-stick silicone paper; grease again and dust with the flour and sugar mixture. Shake off any excess.
2. Remove 2 tablespoons of sugar. Whisk the egg yolks with the remaining sugar until thick, pale and creamy. Mix in the lemon zest.
3. Beat the egg whites until they hold firm snowy peaks and whisk in the reserved sugar.
4. With a large metal spoon mix 2 tablespoons of the beaten egg white into the egg yolk mixture, then lightly fold in the rest in batches, alternating with dredgings of sifted flour. Take care not to beat so as to retain as much air as possible in the mixture.
5. Turn the batter into the prepared tin. Lightly smooth the surface, rap the tin once on the worktop to disperse any air bubbles, and bake immediately in a preheated oven.
6. When the cake is well risen and browned remove from the oven and leave to stand on a wire rack for 10 minutes, then turn out to finish cooling. Use as directed in the recipe. Ⓐ Ⓕ

Ⓐ Can be prepared 1-2 days in advance. Store in an airtight container until ready for use.
Ⓕ May be frozen for 2-3 months. Defrost at room temperature for 1 hour.

Variation:
For a Chocolate fatless sponge replace 2 tablespoons of flour with 2 tablespoons cocoa and 1 teaspoon instant coffee powder. Sift these into the flour.

Raspberry bagatelle (recipe page 54)

GENOESE SPONGE CAKE

Makes one 24 cm (9½ inch) cake
1 tablespoon flour mixed with 1 tablespoon sugar
120 g (4½ oz) caster sugar
5 eggs, separated
1 teaspoon grated lemon zest
120 g (4½ oz) plain flour, well sifted
120 g (4½ oz) unsalted butter, melted and cooled

Preparation time: 25 minutes
Cooking time: 45 minutes
Oven: 180°C, 350°F, Gas Mark 4

1. Prepare the mixture as for steps 1-4 of the Fatless sponge cake recipe.
2. Fold the melted butter into the mixture in three parts. Bake and cool as for the Fatless sponge cake. Ⓐ Ⓕ

Ⓐ Can be made 2-3 days in advance and stored in an airtight container until ready for use.
Ⓕ May be frozen for 2-3 months. Defrost at room temperature for 1 hour.

DESSERT PANCAKES

Makes twelve 18 cm (7 inch) pancakes
150 g (5 oz) plain flour, sifted
pinch of salt
2 eggs
1 egg yolk
2 tablespoons caster sugar
2 tablespoons melted butter
2 tablespoons brandy or rum
1 teaspoon grated lemon zest
450 ml (¾ pint) milk
lard, for frying

Preparation time: 15 minutes plus resting
Cooking time: 25 minutes

1. With a food processor or liquidizer: place the flour, salt, eggs and egg yolk, sugar, butter, brandy and lemon zest in the bowl or goblet and blend for a few seconds. With the machine running, pour in the milk and blend until smooth and creamy. By hand: place the flour and salt in a mixing bowl and make a well in the centre. Gradually whisk in the eggs, adding the milk at the same time. Stir in the butter, brandy and zest.

2. Cover the batter and chill for 2 hours.
3. Heat an 18 cm (7 inch) frying pan over a medium heat and drop in a teaspoon of lard. When it has coated the surface and begins to smoke, pour off the excess.
4. Immediately pour in a ladleful of batter and tilt the pan to spread the mixture evenly over the base; it should be about 2 mm (1/16 inch) thick.
5 Cook the pancake for about 1 minute, then ease it up gently round the sides with a spatula or palette knife. If the heat is correct the underside should be golden. Flip the pancake and cook the other side for about ½ minute more until it is a speckled golden brown.
6. Slide the cooked pancake on to a plate. If using immediately, cover the plate and keep warm over a pan of simmering water.
7. Prepare 11 more pancakes from the remaining batter, reheating the frying pan each time. Stack the cooked pancakes on the warmed plate as they are prepared. Ⓐ Ⓕ

Ⓐ May be made several hours in advance. Store between layers of greaseproof paper.
Ⓕ Can be frozen for up to 2 months. Pack between layers of greaseproof paper then wrap in foil or polythene. Thaw in wrappings at room temperature.

SAVOURY PANCAKES

Makes twelve 18 cm (7 inch) pancakes
150 ml (¼ pint) soda water
150 ml (¼ pint) milk
2 eggs
½ teaspoon salt
125 g (4½ oz) plain flour, sifted
2 tablespoons melted butter
lard, for frying

Preparation time: 10 minutes plus chilling
Cooking time: 25 minutes

1. With a food processor or liquidizer: place the soda water, milk, eggs and salt in the bowl or goblet and blend for 30 seconds. Add the flour and the butter and blend for 1 minute until very light and creamy. By hand: place the flour and salt in a mixing bowl and make a well in the centre. Break in the eggs and gradually whisk them into the flour, slowly adding the milk and soda water at the same time. Whisk until smooth. Stir in the melted butter and blend well.
2. Cover the batter and chill for 2 hours.
3. Cook the pancakes as for Dessert pancakes.

DESSERT CHEESECAKES

CREMA DI MASCARPONE

75 g (3 oz) raisins or sultanas
5 tablespoons dark rum
2 tablespoons instant coffee powder
2 tablespoons boiling water
400 g (13 oz) cream cheese
100 ml (3½ fl oz) soured cream
90 g (3½ oz) caster sugar
2 eggs, separated
2 egg yolks
90 g (3½ oz) small macaroon biscuits
20 g (¾ oz) Amaretti biscuits
chocolate coffee beans, to decorate

Preparation time: 30 minutes plus soaking and freezing

1. Soak the raisins or sultanas in the rum for 30 minutes. Drain, reserving the rum. Dissolve the coffee powder in the boiling water.
2. Beat the cheese with the soured cream, sugar and egg yolks. Mix in 1 tablespoon of the coffee liquid, the soaked fruits and 3 tablespoons of the reserved rum.
3. Line the bottom of a lightly greased 1 kg (2 lb) loaf tin or large glass bowl with the macaroons and Amaretti biscuits. Mix together the remaining rum and coffee liquid and sprinkle over the biscuits to moisten.
4. Whip the egg whites until stiff and fold them into the cheese mixture. Pour the mixture into the tin, smooth over and freeze for 6 hours. F
5. When ready to serve, turn out of the container on to a plate and decorate with the chocolate coffee beans.

F Can be frozen for up to 1 month. Soften in the refrigerator for 1 hour before serving.

Variation:
For special occasions, Crema di mascarpone can be served with a cold chocolate sauce. Combine 2 tablespoons cocoa, 4 tablespoons golden syrup, 50 g (2 oz) diced butter, 150 ml (¼ pint) milk and ½ teaspoon vanilla essence in a heavy-based saucepan, bring to the boil and cook gently for 2-3 minutes. Chill. Pour a little chocolate sauce on to each serving plate and drop a few blobs of single cream on to it, just off centre. Draw a toothpick or fine skewer through the cream, feathering it into the chocolate sauce. Carefully place a slice of frozen Crema di mascarpone on each plate and serve immediately.

CHOCOLATE AND COFFEE PIE

Serves 8
Almond pastry:
175 g (6 oz) ground almonds
50 g (2 oz) caster sugar
1 egg white
Filling:
175 ml (6 fl oz) single cream
165 g (5½ oz) dark dessert chocolate, broken in pieces
225 g (8 oz) cream cheese,
2 tablespoons Tia Maria or other coffee liqueur
2 teaspoons powdered gelatine, dissolved in 2 tablespoons very hot water
To decorate:
whipped cream (optional)
chocolate coffee beans

Preparation time: 35 minutes plus chilling
Cooking time: 30-35 minutes
Oven: 180°C, 350°F, Gas Mark 4

This pie is best eaten the day it is made as the pastry base loses its crispness very quickly.

1. Put the almonds, sugar and egg white into a mixing bowl and knead to a firm paste. Roll into a ball, cover with cling film and chill for 30 minutes.
2. Roll out and press into a greased 20 cm (8 inch) flan tin, bake blind (page 8) for 25-30 minutes until golden brown. Cool.
3. Meanwhile make the filling. Put the cream and chocolate in a heatproof bowl placed over a pan of simmering water and stir until the chocolate has melted. Do not allow the mixture to boil.
4. Cool the bottom of the pan by dipping it quickly into cold water, then put in the refrigerator to chill for 30 minutes.
5. Beat the chocolate cream mixture to thicken slightly then whisk in the cream cheese and Tia Maria. Beat until smooth. Stir in the dissolved gelatine.
6. Spoon the filling into the pastry shell and smooth over. Chill for 3-4 hours.
7. To serve, decorate with whipped cream and chocolate coffee beans.

FROM THE TOP Crema di mascarpone; Chocolate and coffee pie

TORTA DI RICOTTA

Serves 10-12
450 g (1 lb) ricotta cheese, drained and sieved
150 g (5 oz) caster sugar
2 drops bitter almond essence
7 eggs, separated
150 g (5 oz) ground almonds
1 tablespoon grated orange zest
50 g (2 oz) candied orange peel, chopped
2 tablespoons potato flour, sifted
To decorate (optional):
candied orange peel
angelica pieces
icing sugar

Preparation time: 30 minutes
Cooking time: 50 minutes plus cooling
Oven: 180°C, 350°F, Gas Mark 4

1. Grease a 25 cm (10 inch) springform tin and line the base with non-stick silicone paper.
2. Beat the ricotta cheese with the sugar until creamy; mix in the almond essence. Add the egg yolks, one at a time, beating well between each addition. Mix in the almonds, orange zest and candied peel.
3. Whip the egg whites until stiff and gently fold half into the cheese mixture. Sift the potato flour over and fold in, along with the remaining egg white.
4. Pour the mixture into the prepared tin, rap the tin once on the work top to disperse any air pockets, then bake in a preheated oven for 50 minutes until nicely browned. Cool in the tin on a wire rack.
5. Carefully remove the sides of the tin and set the cake on a serving plate. Decorate if liked with candied orange peel, angelica and icing sugar. Serve with Chilled orange sauce.

CHILLED ORANGE SAUCE

rind of 2 oranges, cut into julienne strips
3 tablespoons water
175 g (6 oz) sugar
85 ml (3 fl oz) orange juice
85 ml (3 fl oz) lemon juice

Preparation time: 30 minutes plus chilling
Cooking time: 35 minutes

1. Blanch the orange peel strips in boiling water for 6 minutes to soften. Set aside.
2. Put the water and sugar in a small pan and dissolve slowly over a low heat; add the orange and lemon juice, bring to the boil and then add the orange peel.
3. Simmer for 20 minutes then chill.

ITALIAN RICOTTA CAKE

Serves 10
150 g (5 oz) potato flour
150 g (5 oz) plain flour
150 g (5 oz) butter, cut into small cubes
1 teaspoon grated lemon zest
2 tablespoons caster sugar
2 egg yolks
1 egg white, lightly beaten
icing sugar, to decorate
Filling:
150 ml (¼ pint) milk
piece of vanilla pod 2.5 cm (1 inch) long, split
2 tablespoons caster sugar
2 egg yolks
1 tablespoon flour
300 g (11 oz) ricotta cheese, drained and sieved
3 eggs, separated
50 g (2 oz) icing sugar, sifted
2 tablespoons chopped candied orange and lemon peel
2 tablespoons Grand Marnier
1 egg yolk, lightly beaten

Preparation time: 50 minutes
Cooking time: 40 minutes plus cooling
Oven: 190°C, 375°F, Gas Mark 5

1. First make the pastry. Sift the flours into a bowl and make a well in the centre. Add the cubed butter and lightly rub the mixture to a fine breadcrumb texture. Stir in the lemon zest and sugar. Add the egg yolks and work the mixture into a smooth dough. Roll into a ball, dust with flour, wrap in cling film or foil and chill for 30 minutes. **A**
2. Grease and flour a 25 cm (9½ inch) springform tin. Reserve a third of the pastry. Roll out the rest and line the tin so that the pastry covers the base and extends about 2.5 cm (1 inch) up the sides. Brush the bottom with the lightly beaten egg white.
3. Roll out the remaining pastry and cut into long strips 5 mm (¼ inch) wide. Reserve.
4. Make the filling. Scald the milk with the vanilla pod then leave to infuse until the milk has cooled. Remove the pod.
5. Beat together the sugar and the egg yolks; sift in the flour and stir to combine. Pour in half of the vanilla milk and beat until well blended.

6. Add the egg mixture to the remaining milk in the pan. Bring to the boil very slowly over a low heat and cook for 4-5 minutes, stirring all the time. Set this custard aside to cool.
7. Mix together the ricotta cheese, egg yolks, icing sugar, candied peel and Grand Marnier, beating well between each addition. Mix in the cooled custard.
8. Whip the egg whites until stiff then fold them into the cheese mixture.
9. Pour the mixture into the pastry shell and gently smooth over. Lay reserved strips of pastry on top in a lattice pattern. Brush with beaten egg yolk. Bake in a preheated oven for 40 minutes until cooked. Cool in the tin on a wire rack. **F**
10. Carefully remove the sides of the tin and set the ricotta cake on a serving plate. Dredge with icing sugar and serve.

A Pastry can be made up to 4 days in advance. Cover and keep chilled until required.
F May be frozen for up to 2 months. Defrost at room temperature for 2 hours.

FROM THE LEFT Torta di ricotta, served with Chilled orange sauce; Italian ricotta cake

FRESH CRANBERRY CHEESECAKE

350 g (12 oz) fresh cranberries, washed, or 330 ml (11 fl oz)
    cranberry jelly
3 large strips orange peel
150 g (5 oz) granulated sugar
100 g (4 oz) light brown sugar
1 tablespoon powdered gelatine dissolved in 8 tablespoons
    orange juice
2 tablespoons grated orange zest
200 g (7 oz) cream cheese
200 g (7 oz) curd cheese
100 ml (4 fl oz) double or whipping cream, whipped
1 Biscuitcrumb base in a 22 cm (8½ inch) springform tin
    (page 7)
julienne strips of orange peel, to decorate

Preparation time: 40 minutes plus chilling

1. If using fresh cranberries, place them in a pan and almost cover with cold water. Add the strips of orange peel. Bring to the boil and simmer for 3-4 minutes until the berries start to pop. Draw off the heat and stir in the granulated sugar. Set aside to cool.
2. To make the filling mix together the light brown sugar, gelatine and orange juice mixture and zest. Add the cheeses and beat very thoroughly until quite stiff.
3. Whip the cream. Reserve 4 tablespoons for decoration and fold the rest into the filling.
4. Sieve the cooked cranberries without crushing the fruit and discard the juice. Remove the strips of orange peel. Spread half the cooked fruit or half the cranberry jelly over the chilled base in the tin. Cover with the filling mixture. Spread the remaining cooked cranberries or cranberry jelly over. Chill for 5-6 hours.
5. Carefully remove the sides of the tin and set the cheesecake on a serving plate. Decorate with the reserved whipped cream and the julienne strips of orange peel.

Using Gelatine
As a rule of thumb, 10 g (¼ oz) or 3 teaspoons powdered gelatine will set 500 ml (18 fl oz) cream. Gelatine should always be measured in level spoonfuls; smooth over each spoonful with a knife to check that you have an exact quantity.
1. Pour 75 ml (3 fl oz) very hot, but not boiling water into a cup. Sprinkle 3 teaspoons of powdered gelatine over and stir to dissolve.
2. If the gelatine has not dissolved entirely by the time the water has cooled, stand the cup in a pan of warm water set over a low heat. Stir until the mixture is quite clear and free of any lumps.
3. Allow to cool to room temperature and trickle slowly into the mixture, beating all the time.

APRICOT CHEESECAKE WITH SOURED CREAM PASTRY

Serves 8
Soured cream pastry:
150 g (5 oz) plain flour, sifted
100 g (4 oz) butter, cubed
1 tablespoon caster sugar
1 egg yolk
1 tablespoon soured cream
Filling:
2 tablespoons ground almonds
450 g (1 lb) fresh apricots, halved and stoned or 750 g (1½
    lb) tinned apricots, well drained, juice reserved
1½ teaspoons ground cinnamon
50 g (2 oz) granulated sugar (if using fresh apricots)
50 g (2 oz) butter
2 eggs yolks
185 g (6½ oz) curd cheese
50 g (2 oz) caster sugar
½ teaspoon grated lemon zest
1 tablespoon double cream
To decorate:
teaspoon arrowroot
whipped cream
flaked toasted almonds

Preparation time: 45 minutes plus chilling and cooling
Cooking time: 1 hour 10 minutes
Oven: 180°C, 350°F, Gas Mark 4

1. Sift the flour into a bowl. Add the butter and lightly rub the mixture to a breadcrumb texture. Mix in the sugar. Add the egg yolk and soured cream and blend to a smooth pliable pastry. Roll into a ball, cover with cling film and chill for one hour.
2. Roll out the pastry and line a greased, 22 cm (8½ inch) springform tin, pushing the pastry 2.5 cm (1 inch) up the sides. Scatter the ground almonds over.
3. Reserve 4 apricot halves for decoration. Pack the rest into the prepared base. Mix together 1 teaspoon of cinnamon and sugar and sprinkle over the apricots (if using tinned fruit omit the sugar).
4. Beat the butter with the egg yolks until light and creamy. Mix in the curd cheese, caster sugar, lemon zest, double cream and remaining cinnamon.
5. Pour the mixture on to the fruit in the tin and bake in a preheated oven for 1 hour 10 minutes. Cool in the tin on a wire rack.
6. Carefully remove the sides of the tin and set the cheesecake on a serving plate. Slice the reserved apricot halves and arrange them on top. Mix 8 tablespoons of the reserved juice with the arrowroot and stir over a low heat until thickened. Glaze the apricots then cool. Decorate with whipped cream and flaked almonds and serve.

BLACKBERRY AND CHEESE TORTE

Serves 8

Sweet shortcrust pastry for a 20 cm (8 inch) springform tin
  (page 8)
1 egg white, lightly beaten, for brushing
400 g (14 oz) blackberries, defrosted if frozen
65 g (2½ oz) caster sugar
65 g (2½ oz) macaroons, coarsely crushed
225 g (8 oz) fromage frais, drained, or curd cheese
2 tablespoons Kirsch
3 tablespoons double cream
2 egg yolks
1 egg white
whipped cream, to decorate

Preparation time: 30 minutes plus chilling
Cooking time: 45 minutes
Oven: 190°C, 375°F, Gas Mark 5

1. Roll out the pastry and line the tin so that the pastry covers the base and extends about 2.5 cm (1 inch) up the sides. Bake blind (page 8), brushing the base with beaten egg white five minutes before the baking is complete.
2. Reserve 50 g (2 oz) blackberries for decoration. Sprinkle 50 g (2 oz) of the sugar over the rest.
3. Scatter half the crushed macaroons over the cooked pastry case and lay the sugared blackberries on top.
4. Beat together the cheese, Kirsch, cream, egg yolks and the remaining sugar. Beat the egg white until stiff and fold in. Pour the mixture into the tin and scatter the remaining crushed macaroons on top.
5. Bake in the preheated oven for 45 minutes. Cool in the tin on a wire rack.
6. To serve, carefully remove the sides of the tin and put the torte on a serving plate. Decorate with whipped cream and the reserved blackberries.

CLOCKWISE FROM BOTTOM Apricot cheesecake with soured cream pastry; Fresh cranberry cheesecake; Blackberry and cheese torte

LEMON CHEESECAKE

Serves 8
4 eggs, separated
225 g (8 oz) sugar
75 ml (3 fl oz) water
1 tablespoon powdered gelatine dissolved in 5 tablespoons hot water
200 ml (7 fl oz) lemon juice, strained
4 teaspoons grated lemon zest
300 g (11 oz) fromage frais, sieved, or curd cheese
1 Biscuitcrumb base in a lined 20 cm (8 inch) springform tin (page 7)
To decorate:
whipped cream
lemon slices
green grapes, halved and pipped

Preparation time: 35 minutes plus chilling

This is an easy to prepare cheesecake with an exceptionally light texture, it makes an ideal dessert to serve after a rich main course.

1. Beat the egg yolks until pale and creamy.
2. In a saucepan dissolve the sugar in 75 ml (3 fl oz) water over a low heat. Turn up the heat and boil the syrup to soft ball stage (113°C/235°F–118°C/245°F or when a small amount dropped into iced water forms a sticky soft ball which loses its shape when removed from the water).
3. Pour the syrup on to the egg yolks in a steady stream, beating all the time. Continue beating until the mixture has cooled. Pour into a large bowl.
4. Stir the dissolved gelatine into the mixture. Stir in the lemon juice and lemon zest, blend well and leave to cool.
5. Fold the cheese into the mixture and set aside until on the point of setting.
6. Whip up the egg whites until stiff then gently fold them into the cheese mixture. Pour the mixture into the prepared tin and gently smooth over. Chill for 3-4 hours. Ⓐ Ⓕ
7. To serve, carefully remove the sides of the tin and set the cheesecake on to a serving plate. Decorate with whipped cream, grapes and lemon slices.

Ⓐ May be prepared up to 2 days in advance and kept chilled until required.
Ⓕ May be frozen for 1 month. Thaw at room temperature for 1 hour before serving.

PINEAPPLE REFRIGERATOR CAKE

Serves 12
2 tablespoons powdered gelatine
175 g (6 oz) sugar
pinch of salt
3 eggs, separated
300 ml (½ pint) milk
1 × 225 g (8 oz can) crushed pineapple in natural juice
650 g (1¼ lb) curd cheese
2 teaspoons grated lemon zest
3 tablespoons lemon juice
300 ml (½ pint) double cream
1 Breadcrumb base in a 24 cm (9½ inch) springform tin (page 7)
To decorate:
150 ml (¼ pint) soured cream
candied pineapple
flaked almonds, toasted
scented geranium leaves (optional)

Preparation time: 50 minutes plus setting and chilling
Cooking time: about 15 minutes

1. In a heatproof mixing bowl, mix together the gelatine, sugar and salt.
2. With a fork, lightly beat the egg yolks with the milk and add to the sugar mixture. Mix in the crushed pineapple.
3. Set the mixing bowl over a pan of simmering water and stir for about 15 minutes until the mixture starts to thicken. Draw off the heat and pour into a large mixing bowl. Set aside to cool.
4. Beat together the curd cheese, lemon zest and lemon juice. Gradually add the cooled pineapple mixture and combine well. Set aside until almost on the point of setting.
5. Beat the egg whites until stiff. Whip the double cream until stiff. Fold alternate spoonfuls of whipped cream and egg white into the cheese mixture. Pour on to the chilled base in the tin and carefully smooth over. Chill for 5 hours. Ⓐ Ⓕ
6. To serve, carefully remove the sides of the tin and set the cheesecake on a serving plate. Gently smooth the soured cream over the surface and decorate with the candied pineapple and toasted almond flakes. For a colourful final touch, arrange a few scented geranium leaves on top as well.

Ⓐ May be prepared 2-3 days in advance. Cover and chill until required.
Ⓕ May be frozen for up to 1 month. Thaw at room temperature for 1 hour.

FROM THE TOP Pineapple refrigerator cake; Lemon cheesecake

COFFEE AND RUM CHEESECAKE

Serves 12

2 tablespoons instant coffee powder
3 tablespoons hot water
100 g (4 oz) dark dessert chocolate, broken in pieces
3 tablespoons dark rum
450 g (1 lb) curd cheese
200 g (7 oz) caster sugar
4 eggs, separated
450 ml (¾ pint) double or whipping cream
50 g (2 oz) walnuts, chopped
2 tablespoons powdered gelatine, dissolved in 5
    tablespoons very hot water
1 Walnut and breadcrumb base in a 28 cm (11 inch)
    springform tin (page 7)
To decorate:
walnut halves
chocolate curls
icing sugar

Preparation time: 1 hour 15 minutes plus setting and chilling

1. Dissolve the coffee in the hot water in a small heatproof bowl. Add the chocolate pieces. Place the bowl over a pan of simmering water and stir until melted. Stir in the rum, take off the heat and cool.
2. Beat together the cheese, half the sugar and the egg yolks. Whip the cream and fold in.
3. Transfer half the mixture to another bowl. Add the chocolate and coffee mixture to one half and combine well. Add the walnuts to the other half and stir in.
4. Beat two-thirds of the dissolved gelatine into the coffee and chocolate mixture and add the rest to the walnut mixture. Set both mixtures aside until they are on the point of setting.
5. Meanwhile whip the egg whites until stiff and whisk in the remaining sugar. Fold half of the beaten egg white into each mixture.
6. Pour the walnut mixture on to the base and smooth over. Gently spoon the chocolate and coffee mixture on top. With a large fork, lightly swirl through both mixtures. Chill the cake for at least 6 hours.
7. To serve, carefully remove the sides of the tin and set the cheesecake on a serving plate. Decorate with the walnut halves, chocolate curls and icing sugar.

CASSATA ALLA SICILIANA

Serves 12

1 day-old Genoese sponge cake (page 11) or 450 g (1 lb)
    Madeira cake, cut into 1 cm (½ inch) slices
4 tablespoons Maraschino or Grand Marnier
225 g (8 oz) whole mixed crystallized fruits
500 g (1 lb) ricotta cheese, drained and sieved
150 ml (¼ pint) single cream
50 g (2 oz) sugar
1 teaspoon ground cinnamon
100g (4 oz) dark dessert chocolate, finely chopped
25 g (1 oz) pistachio nuts, blanched, peeled and chopped
½ teaspoon orange-flower water
Icing:
1 tablespoon lemon juice
250 g (9 oz) icing sugar, sifted
about 5 tablespoons almost boiling water

Trimming the cake slices to fit

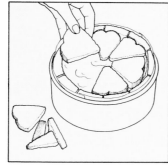
Arranging the slices on top

Preparation time: 1 hour plus chilling

1. Line the base and sides of a 1.75 litre (3 pint) charlotte mould or 18 cm (7 inch) deep cake tin with non-stick silicone paper.
2. Use three-quarters of the cake slices to line the base and sides of the container cutting and trimming to fit (see below). Sprinkle 2 tablespoons of the Maraschino over the cake.
3. Reserve half the crystallized fruits for decoration, finely chop the remainder.
4. Whip the ricotta cheese until creamy then beat in the cream, sugar, cinnamon, chocolate, chopped crystallized fruits and pistachio nuts. Stir in the orange-flower water. Pour into the prepared mould and smooth over. Trim the remaining cake slices and arrange on top, then sprinkle over the remaining Maraschino. Cover and chill for 3-4 hours.
5. Carefully unmould the cake on to serving plate.
6. To make the icing mix the lemon juice with the icing sugar. Stir in tablespoons of hot water until the mixture is thick enough to coat the back of a spoon. Place the bowl over a pan of simmering water and stir until the icing is lukewarm. Pour the icing on to the cake, letting it dribble down the sides. Smooth over with a hot palette knife if necessary.
7. While the icing is still warm decorate with the reserved crystallized fruits. Leave to set then chill. Ⓐ

Ⓐ May be prepared up to 1 day in advance. Cover and keep chilled until required.

HUNGARIAN HOT PANCAKE GÂTEAU

Serves 6

300 g (11 oz) curd cheese
3 eggs, separated
100 g (4 oz) caster sugar
2 tablespoons grated lemon zest
75 g (3 oz) walnuts, ground
2 tablespoons chopped candied or blanched orange peel
12 Dessert pancakes (page 11)
coarsely chopped walnuts, to decorate

Preparation time: 1 hour
Cooking time: 10-15 minutes
Oven: 220°C, 425°F, Gas Mark 7

Filled and rolled pancakes are a well-known dessert, but this layered cheesecake is an unusual variation.

1. Beat the cheese with the egg yolks, sugar and lemon zest. Mix in the ground walnuts and the chopped orange peel. Whip up the egg whites until stiff and lightly fold into the mixture.

2. Spread 1½ tablespoons filling over 11 of the pancakes and layer them in a greased circular ovenproof dish or loose-bottomed cake tin. Lay the remaining pancake on top. Ⓐ Set in a preheated oven for 10-15 minutes.

3. If using a loose-bottomed cake tin, carefully slip off the sides of the tin and set the gâteau on a serving plate. Scatter the gâteau with chopped walnuts and cut in wedges to serve.

Ⓐ The gâteau may be prepared 4-5 hours in advance and cooked immediately before serving.

FROM THE LEFT Coffee and rum cheesecake; Cassata alla Siciliana

BAKED FRESH FRUIT CHEESECAKE

Serves 10
Sweet shortcrust pastry for a 24 cm (9½ inch) springform
  tin (page 8)
20 g (¾ oz) butter, melted
350 g (12 oz) green grapes, halved and pipped
50 g (2 oz) butter
120 g (4½ oz) caster sugar
3 eggs, separated
1 teaspoon grated lemon zest
2 tablespoons double cream
2 tablespoons Kirsch
450 g (1 lb) curd cheese
20 g (¾ oz) cornflour
Topping:
1 egg yolk
2 tablespoons double cream
2 teaspoons caster sugar
2 tablespoons flaked almonds
To decorate:
icing sugar
whole green grapes

Preparation time: 55 minutes plus cooling
Cooking time: about 2 hours
Oven: 200°C, 400°F, Gas Mark 6 (for flan case)
then: 190°C, 375°F, Gas Mark 5 (for cheesecake)

1. Grease the springform tin. Roll out the pastry and
line the tin so that the pastry covers the base and
extends 2.5 cm (1 inch) up the sides. Par-bake for 15-20
minutes (page 8) in a preheated oven. Remove and
reduce the oven temperature.
2. Brush the base of the flan case with melted butter
and arrange the halved grapes on top.
3. Beat together the butter and sugar and mix in the
egg yolks. Add the lemon zest, cream, Kirsch, curd
cheese and cornflour. Mix well.
4. Whip up the egg whites until stiff and fold them into
the cheese mixture. Pour the mixture over the grapes in
the flan case and smooth over.
5. To make the topping, mix together the egg yolk,
double cream and sugar, and spread over the filling.
Sprinkle the flaked almonds on top. Bake in a preheated oven for 1-1¼ hours until golden brown. Cool in
the tin on a wire tray.
6. Carefully remove the sides of the tin. Arrange the
whole grapes on top, dredge with icing sugar and
serve.

Variation:
Any firm fresh fruits may be used instead of grapes:
stoned black cherries, halved and stoned Switzen
plums or cored and coarsely sliced apples and pears.

FROM THE BOTTOM Baked fresh fruit cheesecake; Cherry cheesecake torte

CHERRY CHEESECAKE TORTE

Serves 8
100 g (4 oz) butter
200 g (7 oz) caster sugar
2 eggs, separated
225 g (8 oz) curd cheese
2 teaspoons grated lemon zest
2 tablespoons lemon juice
1 tablespoon powdered gelatine dissolved in 4 tablespoons
  very hot water
150 ml (¼ pint) double or whipping cream
5 tablespoons Kirsch
1 Fatless sponge cake 24 cm (9½ inches) in diameter (page
  10) baked in a deep loose-bottomed tin
1 × 850 g (1½ lb) can pitted morello or black cherries
50 g (2 oz) flaked almonds, toasted
To decorate:
fresh cherries
angelica pieces

Preparation time: 50 minutes plus chilling

Kirsch is an *eau-de-vie* distilled from cherries, and its
traditional combination with chocolate sponge, black
cherries and cream originates in the Black Forest of
Germany. This variation, with the cream cheese filling,
is an unusual alternative. For a more authentic cheesecake use a chocolate sponge base, see page 10.

1. Cream the butter and sugar until light and fluffy,
beat in the egg yolks, one at a time. Beat in the curd
cheese, lemon zest and lemon juice.
2. Stir the dissolved gelatine into the mixture. Leave on
one side until on the point of setting.
3. Whip the egg whites until stiff. Whip the double
cream until stiff. Fold the cream into the cheese
mixture, alternating with spoonfuls of beaten egg
white. Fold in 2 tablespoons of Kirsch.
4. Put the cooled sponge cake back in the cake tin.
Drain the cherries, reserving 3 tablespoons of juice.
Mix the reserved juice with the remaining Kirsch and
sprinkle over the sponge cake to moisten. Scatter the
toasted almond flakes over.
5. Divide the remainder in half. Distribute one half
evenly over the sponge base. Fold the other half into the
filling mixture.
6. Spoon the filling on to the cake in the tin and
carefully smooth over. Chill for 4-5 hours. Ⓐ Ⓕ
7. To serve, carefully remove the sides of the tin and
put the torte on a serving plate. Decorate with the fresh
cherries and angelica pieces.

Ⓐ May be prepared up to 1 day in advance. Cover and
keep chilled until required.
Ⓕ May be frozen for 1 month. Thaw at room temperature for 1 hour before serving.

RUM AND CINNAMON CURD CAKE

Serves 12
1 quantity Yeast dough (page 9)
1 tablespoon melted butter
2 tablespoons toasted breadcrumbs
1 egg yolk, lightly beaten
Rum filling:
25 g (1 oz) butter, softened
3 egg yolks
250 g (9 oz) curd cheese
50 g (2 oz) caster sugar
50 g (2 oz) sultanas
1½ tablespoons double cream
1 tablespoon dark rum
½ teaspoon ground cinnamon
40 g (1½ oz) ground almonds

Preparation time: 1 hour plus rising and cooling
Cooking time: 35-40 minutes
Oven: 190°C, 375°F, Gas Mark 5

1. Put one third of the yeast dough in an oiled plastic bag. Roll out the remaining two-thirds and use to line the base of a greased 26 cm (10½ inch) springform tin. With floured hands gently push the dough about 2 cm (¾ inch) up the sides of the tin.
2. Leave to rise in a warm place, uncovered, for about 20 minutes.
3. Meanwhile make the filling. Beat the butter with the egg yolks until light and creamy. Add the curd cheese and the remaining filling ingredients.
4. Lightly brush the risen dough with melted butter and sprinkle the breadcrumbs over. Spoon in the cheese filling evenly and smooth over.
5. Roll out the remaining pastry dough and cut into long strips 5 mm (¼ inch) wide. Arrange these in a lattice pattern on top of the cake. Brush the pastry with beaten egg yolk.
6. Bake in the preheated oven for 35-40 minutes until golden brown and well risen.
7. Carefully remove the sides of the tin and leave the cake to cool, on its base, on a wire tray. [F]
8. Serve when cool, with pouring cream if liked.

[F] May be frozen for up to 2 months. Defrost at room temperature for 1 hour.

APPLE AND CURD SOUFFLÉ CAKE

Serves 8
1 Breadcrumb base for a 20 cm (8 inch) springform tin (page 7)
450 g (1 lb) Cox's apples
3 tablespoons lemon juice
4 eggs, separated
100 g (4 oz) caster sugar
450 g (1 lb) curd cheese
2 tablespoons grated lemon zest
65 g (2½ oz) potato flour, sifted
1 teaspoon baking powder
4 tablespoons icing sugar

Preparation time: 35 minutes
Cooking time: 1 hour
Oven: 180°C, 350°F, Gas Mark 4

1. Line the base of the springform tin with non-stick silicone paper. Make a collar to fit inside which stands 10 cm (4 inches) higher than the tin. Secure the freestanding part of the collar with sellotape.
2. Press in the prepared breadcrumb base.
3. Peel, core and thinly slice the Cox's apples. Sprinkle them with the lemon juice as you work to prevent discolouration.
4. Whip the egg yolks with the sugar until pale and fluffy; beat in the curd cheese, lemon zest, potato flour and baking powder.
5. Whip the egg whites until stiff and fold them into the cheese mixture.
6. Lay the sliced apples on the crumb base and dredge with 2 tablespoons of icing sugar.
7. Spoon the cheese mixture over and bake in the preheated oven for 1 hour until the cake is well puffed and brown.
8. Take the cake from the oven and carefully remove the sides of the tin and the paper collar. Slide the cake on to a serving dish and dredge with the remaining icing sugar. If liked, pull a knife through the icing sugar to make a lattice pattern on the top of the cake.
9. Serve the cheesecake warm or cold, with pouring cream if liked.

Line the base of the springform tin with a disc of silicone paper

Using 2 pieces of silicone paper make a collar to fit inside the tin

FROM THE LEFT Rum and cinnamon curd cake; Apple and curd soufflé cake

CHILLED LEMON CHEESECAKE

Serves 8

2 tablespoons grated lemon zest
12 tablespoons lemon juice, sieved
100 g (4 oz) light Muscovado sugar
300 g (11 oz) cream cheese
300 g (11 oz) curd cheese
50 g (2 oz) candied orange and lemon peel, chopped
150 ml (¼ pint) double cream, whipped
1 Walnut and breadcrumb base in a 20 cm (8 inch) springform tin (page 7)
lemon slices, to decorate

Preparation time: 20 minutes plus chilling

This refrigerator-set cheesecake has a thick mousse-like texture.

1. Beat together the lemon zest, lemon juice and sugar. Mix in the cheeses and the chopped peel and beat thoroughly. Fold in the whipped cream.
2. Pour the filling on to the base in the tin and smooth over. Chill for 5-6 hours.
3. To serve, carefully remove the sides of the tin and set the cheesecake on a large serving plate. Decorate with lemon slices.

COFFEE & TEATIME CAKES

TRADITIONAL AUSTRIAN BAKED CHEESECAKE

Serves 6
100 g (4 oz) butter
100 g (4 oz) caster sugar
4 eggs, separated
1 teaspoon grated lemon zest
100 g (4 oz) curd cheese
100 g (4 oz) ground almonds
icing sugar, to decorate

Preparation time: 30 minutes
Cooking time: 45 minutes
Oven: 180°C, 350°F, Gas Mark 4

This cake can rise very high on cooking and collapse dramatically as it cools, but still tastes very good!

1. Beat the butter until light and fluffy. Beat in the sugar and egg yolks, one at a time. Mix in the lemon zest, curd cheese and ground almonds.
2. Whip the egg whites until stiff. Whisk 2 tablespoons of beaten egg white into the mixture then fold in the remainder.
3. Pour the mixture into a greased and floured 24 cm (9½ inch) springform tin.
4. Bake in a preheated oven for 45 minutes until well risen and golden. Cool in the tin on a wire tray. Ⓐ Ⓕ
5. Carefully remove the sides of the tin and set the cheesecake on a serving plate. Place a paper doily on top of the cake and sprinkle the icing sugar over. Carefully remove the doily without disturbing the pattern and serve.

Ⓐ May be prepared 2 days in advance. Cover and chill until required.
Ⓕ May be frozen for up to 2 months. Thaw at room temperature for 3-4 hours.

SEVENTEENTH-CENTURY CHEESE TART

Serves 8
300 ml (½ pint) double cream
4 tablespoons sherry
3 eggs
2 egg yolks
50 g (2 oz) caster sugar
2 tablespoons rosewater
¼ teaspoon ground mace
¼ teaspoon ground cinnamon
¼ teaspoon ground nutmeg
½ teaspoon salt
150 g (5 oz) curd cheese
50 g (2 oz) currants
1 Shortcrust pastry case (page 8), baked blind, or Biscuitcrumb base (page 7), in a 20 cm (8 inch) springform tin
To decorate:
icing sugar
crystallized flower petals

Preparation time: 30 minutes plus cooling
Cooking time: 1 hour
Oven: 180°C, 350°F, Gas Mark 4

This cheesecake should be decorated just before serving as the icing sugar has a tendency to soak into the surface of the cheesecake as soon as it is put on.

1. Combine the double cream and sherry in a saucepan and gently heat to just below boiling point. Draw off the heat and set aside.
2. Beat the eggs with the egg yolks, caster sugar rosewater, mace, cinnamon, nutmeg and salt until the mixture is well blended. Beat in the curd cheese. Pour on the scalded cream and sherry in a thin stream, beating all the time. Stir in the currants.
3. Pour the mixture on to the base in the tin and bake in a preheated oven for 1 hour.
4. Cool in the tin on a wire tray. Ⓕ
5. Decorate with sifted icing sugar and crystallized petals and serve.

Ⓕ May be frozen for up to 2 months. Defrost in the refrigerator for 8 hours or overnight.

FROM THE LEFT Traditional Austrian baked cheesecake; Seventeenth-century cheese tart served with coffee topped with whipped cream

CURD CHEESE JAM TART

Serves 8
250 g (9 oz) curd cheese
250 g (9 oz) plain flour, sifted
100 g (4 oz) butter, softened
1 tablespoon caster sugar
pinch of salt
1 egg
250 g (8 oz) plum, gooseberry or damson jam

Preparation time: 35 minutes
Cooking time: 40 minutes
Oven: 180°C, 350°F, Gas Mark 4

This must be eaten the day it is made.

1. Mix together the cheese and the flour. Blend in the butter, sugar and salt. Mix in the egg and knead to a smooth dough.
2. Roll out two-thirds of the pastry on a floured board to a thickness of 1 cm (½ inch). Use to line a greased 26 cm (10½ inch) fluted flan ring. Spread the jam thickly all over the surface.
3. Roll out the rest of the pastry to the same thickness and cut into long strips 1 cm (½ inch) wide. Lay them on top of the tart in a lattice pattern.
4. Bake in the preheated oven for 40 minutes until golden.
5. Serve either warm or cold, with cream.

FROM THE LEFT Curd cheese jam tart; Ginger curd cheese coffyns

GINGER CURD CHEESE COFFYNS

Makes 24

Sweet shortcrust pastry for 24 tartlet shells (page 8)
75 g (3 oz) butter, softened
75 g (3 oz) caster sugar
250 g (9 oz) curd cheese
2 eggs
2 egg yolks
2 tablespoons double cream
1½ teaspoons ground ginger
1 tablespoon grated lemon zest
3 tablespoons currants

Preparation time: 30 minutes
Cooking time: 25 minutes
Oven: 190°C, 375°F, Gas Mark 5

These deliciously rich individual cheesecakes may sound rather ghoulish, but in fact 'coffyn' is an old English word for a pastry case or tartlet shell.

1. Grease and flour 24 deep tartlet moulds. Roll out the pastry, line the moulds and prick the base of each with a fork.
2. Cream the butter and sugar. Beat in the cheese and the eggs and egg yolks, one at a time. Mix in the double cream, ginger, lemon zest and currants.
3. Half fill each tartlet case with the mixture. Bake in a preheated oven for 25 minutes until puffed and golden. Cool on a wire tray in the tartlet moulds.
4. Serve warm or cold. Ⓐ

Ⓐ May be prepared 2-3 days in advance. Cover and chill until required.

CHEESE AND ALMOND CAKE

Serves 6

350 g (12 oz) curd cheese
75 g (3 oz) caster sugar
2 egg yolks
2 teaspoons grated lemon zest
1 tablespoon cornflour
1 tablespoon plain flour
50 g (2 oz) raisins
150 g (5 oz) flaked almonds
4 egg whites
2 tablespoons icing sugar, to decorate

Preparation time: 30 minutes
Cooking time: 40-45 minutes
Oven: 230°C, 450°F, Gas Mark 8
then: 160°C, 325°F, Gas Mark 3

1. Cream the cheese and sugar. Beat in the egg yolks, one at a time, and the lemon zest. Blend thoroughly.
2. Sift in the cornflour and plain flour and add the raisins. Mix well. Reserve 2 tablespoons of flaked almonds and fold the rest into the mixture.
3. Whip the egg whites until stiff and then fold them into the mixture.
4. Pour the mixture into a greased 24 cm (9½ inch) springform tin and scatter the reserved almond flakes over.
5. Place in a preheated oven and reduce the oven temperature. Bake for 40-45 minutes until well risen and brown. *Do not open the oven door* to check the cake until just before the end of the cooking time or it will collapse. Cool in the tin on a wire tray. Ⓐ
6. Just before serving, dredge with icing sugar.

Ⓐ May be prepared 2-3 days in advance. Cover and chill until required.

GRAPE OR PLUM CHEESECAKE

Serves 12

450 g (1 lb) black grapes, halved and pipped, or Switzen
   plums, halved and stoned
1 tablespoon lemon juice
120 g (4½ oz) caster sugar
450 g (1 lb) curd cheese
3 eggs, separated
1 tablespoon grated lemon zest
65 g (2½ oz) potato flour or cornflour
1 teaspoon baking powder
1 Sweet shortcrust pastry case in a 24 cm (9½ inch)
   springform tin (page 8)
To decorate:
whipped cream
black grapes, halved and pipped

Preparation time: 45 minutes
Cooking time: 45 minutes
Oven: 180°C, 350°F, Gas Mark 4

1. Sprinkle the halved grapes with the lemon juice and 1 tablespoon of the caster sugar and set aside.
2. Beat the curd cheese with the remaining caster sugar, then beat in the egg yolks, one at a time, and the lemon zest. Sift the flour with the baking powder and beat into the mixture.
3. Whisk the egg whites until stiff. Beat 3 tablespoons of beaten egg white into the cheese mixture, then carefully fold in the rest, together with the grape halves.
4. Pour the mixture into the pastry lined tin and bake for 45 minutes in the preheated oven, covering towards the end if necessary. Cool in the tin on a wire tray. **F**
5. Carefully remove the sides of the tin and set the cheesecake on a serving plate. Decorate with whipped cream and grape halves and serve.

F May be frozen for up to 3 months. Defrost at room temperature for 3-4 hours.

QUINCE CHEESECAKE

Serves 10
1 Sweet shortcrust pastry case in a 24 cm (9½ inch)
   springform tin (page 8), baked blind
1 egg white, beaten
450 g (1 lb) fresh quinces
2½ tablespoons lemon juice, strained
125 g (4½ oz) granulated sugar
350 ml (12 fl oz) water
50 g (2 oz) caster sugar
1 quantity Soured cream filling (see Simple cheesecake,
   page 35)
icing sugar, to decorate (optional)

Preparation time: 45 minutes
Cooking time: 1 hour 50 minutes
Oven: 180°C, 350°F, Gas mark 4

The edible quince is not to be confused with the hard, small fruits of the spring-flowering japonica. It looks rather like a large handsome pear and has yellow flesh which turns a deep pink colour on cooking, and has a strong sweet perfume and flavour. Quinces are available in the autumn from specialist fruiterers. When quinces are out of season you can use raw apples instead.

1. Brush the cooked pastry case with beaten egg white.
2. Peel, core and slice the quinces. Reserving the peel and cores. Place the quince slices in a bowl, cover with water and add ½ tablespoon of the lemon juice.
3. Put the quince trimmings, remaining lemon juice, granulated sugar and water in a saucepan. Boil for 30 minutes until thick and syrupy. Strain the syrup and return to the rinsed pan.
4. Drain the quince slices and add to the pan. Poach in the syrup for 30 minutes until softened but not soggy. Drain and leave to cool.
5. Arrange the quince slices over the base of the pastry case. Dredge the caster sugar over.
6. Pour the Soured cream filling over the quince slices in the tin. Place in a preheated oven and bake for 50 minutes until well golden. Cool in the tin on a wire tray.
7. Carefully remove the sides of the tin. Set the cake on a serving plate, dredge with icing sugar, if liked, and serve.

CHEESECAKE WITH APPLES

Makes 30 slices
Sweet shortcrust pastry for a 24-26 cm (9½-10½ inch) tin
   (page 8)
250 g (9 oz) curd cheese
50 g (2 oz) caster sugar
2 egg yolks
1 egg
2 teaspoons grated lemon zest
100 g (4 oz) butter, melted
50 g (2 oz) toasted breadcrumbs
1 tablespoon ground cinnamon
1 kg (2 lb) Bramley apples, peeled, cored and cut into 3 mm
   (⅛ inch) slices
65 g (2½ oz) icing sugar, sifted
300 ml (½ pint) soured cream
2 tablespoons caster sugar
1 tablespoon orange juice, strained
icing sugar, to decorate

Preparation time: 45 minutes
Cooking time: 50 minutes
Oven: 190°C, 375°F, Gas Mark 5

Although these cheesecake slices look rather unspectacular, they taste absolutely delicious!

1. Roll out the pastry dough and line 2 baking trays, 20 × 28 × 4 cm (8 × 11 × 1½ inches). Prick all over with a fork. Chill.
2. To make the filling, beat together the cheese, sugar, egg yolks, whole egg and lemon zest.
3. Brush the pastry with a little melted butter. Mix together the toasted breadcrumbs and cinnamon and scatter over the pastry.
4 Divide the filling equally between both trays and smooth over.
5. Arrange an even layer of apples over the filling on each tray; dredge with icing sugar and sprinkle the rest of the melted butter over.
6. Mix the soured cream with the sugar and orange juice. Spoon half of it over the apple slices.
7. Bake in the preheated oven for 35 minutes. Remove from the oven and spread the rest of the soured cream mixture over. Replace in the oven and bake for a further 15 minutes. Cool in the tins on wire trays. Ⓐ Ⓕ
8. When cool, cut the cheesecake in each tray into rectangular pieces and dust with icing sugar before serving.

Ⓐ May be prepared 1 day in advance. Cover the trays with clingfilm or tin foil and keep cool.
Ⓕ May be frozen for up to 2 months. Thaw uncovered at room temperature for 1 hour.

FROM THE LEFT Grape or plum cheesecake; Quince cheesecake

CASSATINE DI RICOTTA
Ricotta Tartlets

Makes 20
150 ml (¼ pint) milk
piece of vanilla pod 2.5 cm (1 inch) long
2 egg yolks
2 tablespoons caster sugar
1 tablespoon plain flour
75 g (3 oz) unsalted butter, softened
90 g (3½ oz) ricotta cheese, drained, or curd cheese
2 tablespoons dark rum
20 Sweet shortcrust pastry tartlet shells, baked blind
(page 8)
To decorate:
angelica pieces or halved glacé cherries

Preparation time: 40 minutes
Cooling time: 5 minutes

These individual Italian tarts are unusual in that their rum/vanilla filling is uncooked.

1. Put the milk and vanilla pod in a small pan and heat to just below boiling point. Take off the heat and set aside to cool. Remove the vanilla pod.
2. Put the egg yolks and sugar in another pan and beat together. Blend in the flour. Slowly pour on the scalded milk, beating all the time; place over a gentle heat and stir until thickened. Draw the custard off the heat and leave to cool.
3. In a large mixing bowl beat the butter until creamy then blend in the ricotta cheese. Beat in the cooled custard a little at a time, then stir in the rum.
4. Spoon the mixture into the tartlet cases and smooth over. Chill.
5. Place a piece of angelica on top of each tartlet and serve immediately.

MAIDS OF HONOUR

Makes 15
Shortcrust pastry for 15 deep tartlet shells (page 8)
120 g (4½ oz) curd cheese
90 g (3½ oz) butter
2 egg yolks
2 tablespoons brandy
90 g (3½ oz) caster sugar
90 g (3½ oz) ground almonds
pinch of ground nutmeg
1 tablespoon lemon juice
1 teaspoon grated lemon zest

GREEK HONEY CHEESECAKE

Serves 8
Sweet shortcrust pastry for a 22 cm (8½ inch) springform
  tin (page 8)
200 g (7 oz) curd cheese
150 ml (¼ pint) double cream
50 ml (2 fl oz) flower-flavoured honey
3 tablespoons caster sugar
1 teaspoon ground cinnamon
2 teaspoons grated lemon zest
½ teaspoon ground nutmeg
2 eggs, lightly beaten
To decorate:
whipped cream
lemon slices

Preparation time: 30 minutes
Cooking time: 1 hour
Oven: 180°C, 350°F, Gas Mark 4

1. Roll out the pastry and line the tin so that the pastry covers the base and extends 2½ cm (1 inch) up the sides. Heat the oven and place a baking sheet on the middle shelf.
2. Beat together the cheese and the cream. Mix in the honey, 2 tablespoons of the sugar, ½ teaspoon of the cinnamon, the lemon zest and nutmeg. Beat in the eggs, one at a time.
3. Pour the mixture into the prepared pastry case. Mix together the remaining sugar and cinnamon and sprinkle over.
4. Stand the tin on the hot baking sheet in the preheated oven and bake for 1 hour until risen and golden. Cool in the tin on a wire tray.
5. Carefully remove the sides of the tin and set the cake on a serving plate. Decorate with rosettes of whipped cream and lemon slices and serve.

Preparation time: 40 minutes plus cooling
Cooking time: about 25 minutes
Oven: 200°C, 400°F, Gas Mark 6

1. Grease 10 deep tartlet moulds and line with the pastry. Prick the base of each with a fork.
2. Beat the curd cheese with the butter until smooth, add the egg yolks, one at a time, the brandy, caster sugar and ground almonds. Mix in the nutmeg, lemon juice and lemon zest.
3. Half fill each tartlet case and bake in a preheated oven for 25 minutes until puffed and golden. Cool in the shells on a wire tray. Serve.

ROLLED CHEESECAKE

Serves 8

250 g (9 oz) plain flour
1 teaspoon baking powder
2 tablespoons butter, chilled and cubed
50 g (2 oz) caster sugar
1 egg yolk
up to 100 ml (3½ oz) milk
50 g (2 oz) butter
50 g (2 oz) caster sugar
1 tablespoon vanilla sugar
250 g (9 oz) curd cheese
65 g (2 oz) hazelnuts, toasted and ground
50 g (2 oz) sultanas
1 egg, lightly beaten
2 tablespoon icing sugar, to serve

Preparation time: 30 minutes
Cooking time: 45 minutes
Oven: 190°C, 375°F, Gas Mark 5

1. Sift the flour with the baking powder into a mound on the worktop.
2. Add the butter and rub to a fine breadcrumb texture. Mix in the sugar. Add the egg yolk and enough milk to produce a firm smooth dough. Roll out the pastry into a rectangle 45 × 30 cm (18 × 12 inches).
3. To make the filling, beat the butter until light and creamy. Beat in the caster sugar, vanilla sugar and curd cheese.
4. Spread the filling over the pastry, leaving a 2 cm (1 inch) border of pastry around the edge. Scatter the ground hazelnuts and sultanas over.
5. Fold in the pastry border and carefully roll up from the long side.
6. Transfer to a greased baking sheet, seam side down, curling the roll if necessary. Brush with beaten egg and bake for 45 minutes. Cool on a wire tray. Ⓐ
7. Dredge with icing sugar and serve in slices.

Ⓐ May be prepared up to 2 days in advance. Cover and chill until required.

SAFFRON CHEESECAKE

Serves 10
1 pinch saffron strands
1 teaspoon lemon juice
400 g (14 oz) curd cheese
150 g (5 oz) caster sugar
3 egg yolks
2 tablespoons ground almonds
1 tablespoon grated lemon zest
25 g (1 oz) plain flour, sifted
100 ml (3½ fl oz) soured cream
2 tablespoons butter, melted
150 g (5 oz) sultanas
3 egg whites
1 Sweet shortcrust pastry case in a 24 cm (9½ inch)
  springform tin, 2½ cm (1 inch) deep, baked blind
  (page 8)
1 tablespoon ground cinnamon, to decorate

FROM THE LEFT Rolled cheesecake; Saffron cheesecake; Simple cheesecake

**Preparation time: 30 minutes plus soaking
Cooking time: 1 hour 10 minutes
Oven: 180°C, 350°F, Gas Mark 4**

An old-fashioned baked cheesecake with a subtle flavour of saffron and almonds.

1. Soak the saffron in the lemon juice for 1 hour.
2. Beat the curd cheese with the caster sugar and egg yolks.
3. Mix in the ground almonds, lemon zest and flour, then beat in the soured cream, melted butter, saffron liquid and sultanas.
4. Whip the egg whites until stiff and gently fold them into the mixture.
5. Pour the filling into the cooked pastry shell and smooth over. Bake in a preheated oven for 1 hour 10 minutes until well risen and set. Cool in the tin on a wire tray.
6. Lay a doily over the cake and sprinkle with cinnamon. Remove the doily and serve.

SIMPLE CHEESECAKE

Serves 8
450 g (1 lb) curd cheese
150 ml (¼ pint) soured cream
3 eggs, separated
175 g (6 oz) caster sugar
2 teaspoons grated lemon zest
Sweet shortcrust pastry case in a 22 cm (8½ inch)
  springform tin, baked blind (page 8)
To decorate:
fresh soft fruits e.g. strawberries, raspberries, redcurrants
  (optional)
icing sugar

**Preparation time: 30-40 minutes, plus cooling
Cooking time: 45-55 minutes
Oven: 180°C, 350°F, Gas Mark 4**

1. Beat the curd cheese with the soured cream, egg yolks and caster sugar until thick and creamy. Mix in the lemon zest.
2. Whip the egg whites until stiff and fold them into the mixture. Pour the mixture into the cooked pastry case and bake in a preheated oven for 45-55 minutes. Cool in the tin on a wire tray, **A** **F**
3. Arrange the fruit on top of the cheesecake, dredge with icing sugar and serve.

A May be prepared up to 3 days in advance. Cover and chill until required.
F May be frozen for up to 2 months. Thaw at room temperature for 3-4 hours.

CURD AND CHOCOLATE GUGELHOPF

Serves 10
150 g (5 oz) butter, softened
150 g (5 oz) caster sugar
3 egg yolks
150 g (5 oz) plain flour
1 teaspoon baking powder
1 tablespoon Tia Maria or dark rum
2 tablespoons icing sugar, to decorate
Filling:
250 g (9 oz) curd cheese
2 egg yolks
50 g (2 oz) caster sugar
1 tablespoon soured cream
2 tablespoons cocoa powder
2 tablespoons Tia Maria or dark rum
melted butter, for brushing

Preparation time: 30 minutes
Cooking time: 1 hour 10 minutes
Oven: 180°C, 350°F, Gas Mark 4

STRUDEL CHEESE ROLL

Serves 10
50 g (2 oz) butter, softened
50 g (2 oz) caster sugar
2 egg yolks
300 g (11 oz) curd cheese
120 ml (4 fl oz) double cream
1 teaspoon grated lemon zest
50 g (2 oz) sultanas
50 g (2 oz) chopped walnuts
225 g (8 oz) filo pastry (12 sheets, see page 73)
120 g (4½ oz) unsalted butter, melted
icing sugar, to decorate

Preparation time: 45 minutes
Cooking time: 40 minutes
Oven: 190°C, 375°F, Gas Mark 5

Gugelhopf is a traditional cake which originated in Austria. It is baked in an unusual tin which has fluted slanting sides and a central funnel, although a ring mould may be used instead.

1. Cream together the butter and sugar until light and fluffy. Beat in the egg yolks one at a time.
2. Sift the flour with the baking powder and beat thoroughly into the main mixture, 2 tablespoons at a time. Mix in the Tia Maria.
3. To make the filling, blend the curd cheese with the egg yolks and the caster sugar. Beat in the soured cream, sift in the cocoa and mix in the Tia Maria.
4. Brush a 23 cm (9 inch) gugelhopf mould very thoroughly with melted butter.
5. Spoon half of the flour mixture into the tin. Spoon in the filling, then spoon in the remaining flour mixture.
6. Bake in a preheated oven for 1 hour 10 minutes until it is well risen and shrinking away from the sides of the tin. Rest in the tin for 10 minutes before transferring to a wire tray to cool.
7. Dredge with icing sugar to serve.

1. To make the filling, beat the butter with the sugar until light and fluffy. Beat in the egg yolks, one at a time and the curd cheese. Beat in the double cream and lemon zest. Fold in the sultanas and chopped walnuts.
2. Lay a clean tea towel on a work top. Lay a sheet of filo pastry on it and brush with melted butter. Lay another sheet next to it, overlapping by 6 cm (2½ inches). Lay the remaining 10 sheets on top, in the same way brushing each one with melted butter, reserving some melted butter for the finished strudel.
3. Spread the filling over the sheets of filo, leaving a 5 cm (2 inch) border of pastry around the edge.
4. Fold in the pastry border and carefully roll the strudel up from the short end.
5. Transfer, seam side down, to a greased baking sheet. Brush with the remaining melted butter and bake in a preheated oven for 40 minutes until puffed and golden.
6. Serve warm or cold, dredged with icing sugar.

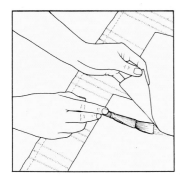

Brushing the sheets of filo pastry with melted butter

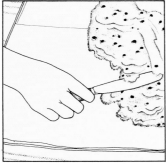

Spreading the filling over the filo layers, leaving a border all round

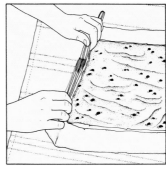

Folding in the pastry border

Rolling up the strudel, using the tea towel as an aid

FROM THE TOP Curd and chocolate gugelhopf; Strudel cheese roll

BLUEBERRY AND CREAM CHEESE PIE

Serves 6
225 g (8 oz) cream cheese
1 tablespoon soured cream
2 tablespoons lemon juice, strained
2 tablespoons grated lemon zest
75 g (3 oz) icing sugar sifted
3 eggs, lightly beaten
1 Sweet shortcrust pastry base in a 23 cm (9 inch)
   springform tin, baked blind (page 8)
Topping:
225 g (8 oz) blueberries, defrosted if frozen
50 g (2 oz) sugar
1 tablespoon arrowroot
pinch of salt
2 tablespoons lemon juice, strained
whipped cream, to decorate (optional)

**Preparation time: 50 minutes plus cooking and
chilling
Cooking time: 50 minutes
Oven: 180°C, 350°F, Gas Mark 4**

SOURED CREAM CHEESECAKE

Serves 8
450 g (1 lb) curd cheese
75 g (3 oz) caster sugar
1 teaspoon vanilla essence
3 eggs
1 Walnut and breadcrumb base in a 22 cm (8½ inch)
   springform tin (page 7)
julienne strips of orange peel, to decorate
Topping:
2 tablespoons vanilla sugar
1 tablespoon fresh orange juice
1 tablespoon grated orange zest
300 ml (½ pint) soured cream
julienne strips of orange peel, to decorate

**Preparation time: 40 minutes plus chilling
Cooking time: 40 minutes
Oven: 200°C, 400°F, Gas Mark 6**

1. Beat the curd cheese with the caster sugar and
vanilla essence. Beat in the eggs one at a time and
combine well.
2. Pour on to the prepared crumb base and bake for 20
minutes. Cool in the tin on a wire tray.
3. Thoroughly combine the topping ingredients, and
pour on to the cooked cheesecake in the tin. Smooth
over with a palette knife then bake in a preheated oven
for 20 minutes until set. Cool in the tin on a wire tray.
Chill well.
4. Carefully remove the sides of the tin, decorate with
orange peel and serve.

1. Beat together the cheese, soured cream, lemon juice
and lemon zest until smooth. Whisk in the icing sugar
and beaten eggs until light and creamy.
2. Pour the filling on to the pastry base in the tin and
bake in a preheated oven for 40 minutes until just set.
Cool in the tin on a wire tray.
3. Meanwhile make the topping. Strain the blueberries, reserving the juice, and place them in a pan
with the sugar, arrowroot and salt. Add the lemon juice
to the reserved juice, measure, and make up 150 ml
(¼ pint) with cold water. Add to the pan.
4. Bring the mixture to a gentle simmer and cook for
about 3 minutes until the syrup is smooth, clear and
thick. Remove and leave to cool for 10 minutes.
5. Pour the topping over the cooked cheese filling and
smooth over. Chill for at least 4 hours. **A**
6. To serve, carefully remove the sides of the tin and set
the cake on a serving plate. Decorate, if liked, with
whipped cream.

A May be prepared 2-3 days in advance. Cover and
chill until required.

PECAN CHEESECAKE

Serves 10

500 g (1¼ lb) curd cheese
200 g (7 oz) caster sugar
pinch of salt
1 tablespoon vanilla sugar
1 teaspoon grated lemon zest
4 eggs, separated
120 ml (4 fl oz) double cream
65 g (2½ oz) plain flour, sifted
1 Pecan nut and breadcrumb base in a 22 cm (8½ inch)
   springform tin (page 7)

To decorate:
whipped cream
pecan halves

Preparation time: 40 minutes plus cooling
Cooking time: 1 hour
Oven: 160°C, 325°F, Gas mark 3

1. Mix the curd cheese with 100 g (3½ oz) of the sugar, the salt, vanilla sugar and lemon zest. Blend in the egg yolks, one at a time.

2. Whip the egg whites until stiff. Beat in the remaining caster sugar, a tablespoon at a time, and continue beating until very firm. Lightly whip the double cream and fold in, with the flour. Fold this mixture into the cheese mixture.

3. Pour the mixture on to the pecan base in the tin and smooth over. Bake for 1¼ hours. Cool in the tin or on a wire tray. Chill. **F**

4. Carefully remove the sides of the tin and set the cheesecake on a serving plate. Pipe with fresh cream rosettes, arrange the pecan halves around the edge on top of the cream. Serve.

F May be frozen for 4-6 weeks. Defrost, uncovered, at room temperature for 2 hours before serving.

FROM THE LEFT Soured cream cheesecake; Blueberry and cream cheese pie; Pecan cheesecake

CELEBRATION CAKES

CHEESECAKE AND FRUIT DIPLOMAT

Serves 14-16
Cheesecake ring:
350 g (12 oz) ricotta or cottage cheese, drained and sieved
75 g (3 oz) caster sugar
3 eggs, separated
1 tablespoon grated orange zest
1 teaspoon grated lemon zest
2 tablespoons lemon juice, strained
150 ml (¼ pint) soured cream
1 tablespoon powdered gelatine, dissolved in
　　2 tablespoons very hot water
150 ml (¼ pint) double cream
Fruit base:
3 tablespoons apricot jam
1 Fatless sponge cake, quantity as for page 10 but baked
　　in a 30 cm (12 inch) springform tin
750 g (1½ lb) prepared fresh fruit or drained canned fruit
　　(see below)
To serve:
julienne strips of orange and lemon peel
double quantity Chilled orange sauce (page 14)

Preparation time: 1 hour plus chilling
Cooking time: 3 minutes

HEAVENLY CAKE

Serves 12
1 quantity Cinnamon pastry (see Chocolate truffle torte,
　　page 44)
2 tablespoons flaked almonds
250 g (8 oz) cranberry or redcurrant jelly
1 quantity Cheese cream filling (see Fresh strawberry
　　cake, page 47)
whole fresh fruit (redcurrants, raspberries), to decorate

Preparation time: 80 minutes plus chilling (see
Chocolate truffle torte page 44)
Cooking time: 30 minutes
Oven: 180°C, 350°F, Gas Mark 4

You can use virtually any combination of fruit for this spectacular party dessert: peaches, pears, apricots, gooseberries, black cherries, or red and black currants. Choose fruits which complement each other well in colour and texture.

1. To make the Cheesecake ring beat the cheese, sugar and egg yolks together thoroughly. Beat in the orange and lemon zest, lemon juice and soured cream.
2. Slowly beat in the dissolved gelatine. Put the mixture to one side until on the point of setting.
3. Whip the egg whites until stiff and lightly whip the double cream. Fold alternate spoonfuls of egg white and whipped cream into the stiffened mixture.
4. Pour the mixture into a lightly oiled 24 cm (9 inch) ring mould. Chill for 3-4 hours.
5. Meanwhile, gently heat the apricot jam with 3 tablespoons of water and stir to dissolve. Sieve.
6. Place the sponge cake on a large serving plate and brush with the melted apricot jam. Carefully unmould the cheesecake on top, leaving an even edge all around.
7. Arrange some of the fruits decoratively around the edge of the cheesecake. Place the remaining fruit in the centre of the cheesecake. Chill for 2 hours.
8. Decorate with the julienne strips of peel and serve with the Chilled orange sauce.

This is a summer version of the Chocolate truffle torte (page 44) and is much lighter and less rich. It also needs to be chilled for 2 days before serving.

1. Roll out and bake the pastry rounds as for Chocolate truffle torte, scattering the flaked almonds over 1 round before baking. Cool on wire trays.
2. Set the almond-coated round to one side. Spread a layer of jelly over each of the remaining pastry rounds, then spread each one with a layer of Cheese cream filling.
3. Sandwich the 3 layers together and set the almond-coated layer on top. Chill for 2 days.
4. Garnish with fresh fruit and serve.

FROM THE TOP Cheesecake and fruit diplomat with Chilled orange sauce; Heavenly cake

BLACKCURRANT AND ORANGE CHEESECAKE

Serves 10

1 Breadcrumb base in a 26 cm (10½ inch) springform tin (page 7)
1 Fatless sponge cake 26 cm (10½ inches) in diameter (page 10)
6 tablespoons cranberry jelly
1 × 400 g (14 oz) jar or can blackcurrants
3 tablespoons Cointreau
Filling:
350 g (12 oz) curd cheese
75 g (3 oz) caster sugar
3 eggs, separated
2 tablespoons grated orange zest
2 tablespoons orange juice, strained
4 teaspoons powdered gelatine, dissolved in 3 tablespoons very hot water
300 ml (½ pint) double cream
To decorate:
julienne strips of orange peel
chopped pistachio nuts
whipped cream

Preparation time: 1 hour 30 minutes plus chilling
Cooking time: 3 minutes

1. To make the filling, cream together the curd cheese and sugar. Beat in the egg yolks, one at a time, the orange zest and the orange juice. Beat in the dissolved gelatine and put the mixture to one side until on the point of setting.
2. Gently heat the cranberry jelly with 2 tablespoons of water and stir to dissolve. Cool.
3. Brush the breadcrumb base with the melted cranberry jelly. Lay the sponge cake on top.
4. Drain the blackcurrants, reserving the juice. Mix 6 tablespoons of juice with the Cointreau and sprinkle over the sponge cake. Arrange the blackcurrants on top, reserving some for decoration.
5. Lightly whip the cream. Beat the egg whites until stiff and fold into the mixture, alternating with spoonfuls of whipped cream.
6. Pour the filling over the fruit in the tin and chill for 5-6 hours until set. Ⓐ
7. To serve, carefully remove the sides of the tin and set the cheesecake on a serving plate. Decorate with the reserved blackcurrants, orange peel, chopped pistachio nuts and whipped cream.

Ⓐ Can be prepared up to 3 days in advance. Cover and chill until ready to decorate and serve.

CHILLED STRAWBERRY CAKE

Serves 8

1 Shortcrust pastry base 22 cm (8½ inches) in diameter, baked blind (page 8)
Filling:
350 g (12 oz) strawberries, defrosted if frozen
3 tablespoons Kirsch
120 g (4½ oz) caster sugar
450 g (1 lb) curd cheese
3 eggs, separated
100 ml (3½ fl oz) soured cream
2 tablespoons powdered gelatine dissolved in 5 tablespoons very hot water
To decorate:
whipped cream
toasted almond flakes

Preparation time: 30 minutes plus soaking and chilling

1. Lightly oil a 22 cm (8½ inch) springform tin and line the base and sides with non-stick silicone paper. Place the pastry base in the tin.
2. Reserve 6 strawberries (with stalks if possible) for decoration. Hull the rest, gently mix with the Kirsch and sugar and leave to soak for 1-2 hours.
3. Strain the strawberries, reserving the liquid. Put the curd cheese in a large mixing bowl. Pass the strawberries through a nylon sieve on to the cheese. Blend well.
4. Beat in the egg yolks, one at a time, then slowly beat in the reserved strawberry liquid. Mix in the soured cream and the dissolved gelatine. Put to one side until on the point of setting.
5. Whip the egg whites until stiff and fold them into the filling mixture. Pour the mixture into the tin and chill for 5-6 hours. Ⓐ Ⓕ
6. Gently slide off the sides of the tin and remove the side pieces of silicone paper. Set the cake on a serving plate. Smooth whipped cream over the top and decorate with rosettes of cream, the reserved strawberries and toasted almond flakes. Serve.

Ⓐ May be prepared up to 3 days in advance. Cover and keep chilled until required.
Ⓕ May be frozen for up to 2 months. Thaw for 1 hour at room temperature.

Variation:
If preferred raspberries, or even a combination of half raspberries and half strawberries, may be used for this cheesecake. In both cases, substitute framboise liqueur for the Kirsch.

FROM THE LEFT Blackcurrant and orange cheesecake; Chilled strawberry cake; Summer meringue cheesecake

SUMMER MERINGUE CHEESECAKE

Serves 8
Meringue:
4 egg whites
225 g (8 oz) caster sugar
Filling:
1 quantity Cheese cream filling (see Fresh strawberry cake, page 47)
100 g (4 oz) fresh redcurrants
350 g (12 oz) fresh raspberries
To decorate:
1 egg white
1 tablespoon sugar

Preparation time: 35 minutes
Cooking time: 1½ hours
Oven: 140°C, 275°F, Gas Mark 1

1. Draw two 24 cm (9½ inch) circles on sheets of non-stick silicone paper and place the sheets on baking trays.
2. Whisk the egg whites until they hold firm snowy peaks; sift in half the sugar and beat lightly for a few seconds until the mixture is satiny smooth. Sift over the remaining sugar and fold in.
3. Spoon half the meringue mixture into each circle and smooth over lightly. Bake in a preheated oven for about 1½ hours until dry and crisp. Cool on wire trays. **A**
4. Set one meringue base on a serving plate and spread half the cheese cream filling on top. Reserve a few redcurrants (with stalks if possible) and raspberries for decoration, arrange the rest evenly over the filling. Spread the remaining filling over the fruit and top with the second meringue layer.
5. Lightly beat the egg white. Dip the reserve redcurrants first in egg white and then in sugar to frost. Leave to dry.
6. Arrange the frosted redcurrants and reserved raspberries on top of the cake and serve immediately, before the raspberry juices run into the filling.

A The meringue layers may be made 2 weeks in advance and kept in an airtight container until required. The filling may be prepared 1 day in advance and chilled until required. Assemble the cheesecake just before serving.

HAZELNUT AND CHOCOLATE CHEESECAKE

Serves 12-14

120 g (4½ oz) plain chocolate 'thins' (about 18)
1 Hazelnut and breadcrumb base in a 26 cm (10½ inch) oiled springform tin (page 7)
Filling:
75 g (3 oz) plain dessert chocolate, broken in pieces
2 tablespoons hot water
450 g (1 lb) curd cheese
4 eggs, separated
150 g (5 oz) caster sugar
4 tablespoons dark rum
300 ml (½ pint) double cream
4 teaspoons powdered gelatine dissolved in 4 tablespoons very hot water
75 g (3 oz) toasted hazelnuts, chopped
To decorate:
whole toasted hazelnuts
whipped cream

Preparation time: 50 minutes plus chilling
Cooking time: 5 minutes

1. Arrange the chocolate 'thins' upright around the edge of the springform baking tin, pressing them lightly into the prepared base for support. Chill.
2. Meanwhile put the chocolate and water in a heatproof bowl placed over a pan of simmering water and stir until the chocolate has melted. Allow to cool.
3. Beat the curd cheese with the egg yolks then beat in the sugar, melted chocolate, rum and double cream. Stir in the dissolved gelatine and put the mixture to one side until on the point of setting.
4. Whip the egg whites until stiff and lightly fold them into the stiffened cheese mixture with the chopped hazelnuts.
5. Pour the mixture into the chocolate-lined tin and smooth over. Chill for 5-6 hours until set. Ⓐ
6. Gently remove the sides of the tin and set the cheesecake on a serving plate. Decorate with hazelnuts and whipped cream. Serve.

Ⓐ May be prepared up to 3 days in advance, covered and kept chilled until required.

CHOCOLATE TRUFFLE TORTE

Serves 12
Cinnamon pastry:
5 teaspoons ground cinnamon
275 g (10 oz) caster sugar
120 g (4½ oz) butter, softened
4 egg yolks
2 teaspoons grated lemon zest
250 g (9 oz) plain flour
pinch of baking powder
Filling:
275 g (10 oz) dark dessert chocolate, broken in pieces
175 ml (6 fl oz) double cream
150 g (5 oz) curd cheese
2 tablespoons dark rum
450 ml (¾ pint) whipping cream
To decorate:
flaked toasted almonds
chocolate coffee beans

Preparation time: 1 hour plus cooling and chilling (see below)
Cooking time: 50 minutes
Oven: 180°C, 350°F, Gas Mark 4

This is a very rich cheesecake. For best results it should be chilled for 2 days before serving.

1. To make the pastry, mix the cinnamon with half of the sugar and reserve.
2. Beat the butter with the remaining sugar until light and fluffy. Beat in the egg yolks and the lemon zest.
3. Sift the flour with the baking powder and blend into the mixture. Knead until smooth and well blended.
4. Divide the pastry in 4 and press or roll out each piece into a 24 cm (9½ inch) round (as a guide, cut around the base of a springform tin). Sprinkle the cinnamon and sugar mixture over the pastry rounds.
5. Bake the rounds on a greased baking sheet for 15 minutes in a preheated oven. Cool on wire trays.
6. To make the filling, melt the chocolate in a small heatproof bowl over a pan of simmering water. Cool.
7. Gently heat the double cream in a saucepan to just below boiling point. Draw off the heat and gradually beat in the melted chocolate. Leave to cool.
8. Beat the chocolate cream until doubled in bulk. Beat in the curd cheese and rum.
9. Reserve 8 tablespoons of chocolate cream. Spread the remainder over 3 of the pastry rounds.
10. Whip the whipping cream until stiff. Reserve 3 tablespoons for decoration and spread the remainder over the 3 chocolate-covered pastry rounds. Sandwich the 3 layers together.
11. Spread some of the reserved chocolate cream over the remaining pastry round and place on top of the other layers. Pipe with contrasting rosettes of chocolate cream and whipped cream and decorate with chocolate coffee beans and flaked almonds. Chill.

HAZELNUT CHEESE GALETTE

Serves 8

100 g (4 oz) butter, diced
150 g (5 oz) flour, sifted
75 g (3 oz) caster sugar
75 g (3 oz) toasted hazelnuts, ground
1 quantity Cheese cream filling (see Fresh strawberry
  cake, page 47) made with framboise liqueur
350 g (12 oz) raspberries, defrosted if frozen
whipped cream, to decorate (optional)

Preparation time: 45 minutes
Cooking time: 10-15 minutes
Oven: 160°C, 325°F, Gas Mark 3

1. Place the butter and flour in a mixing bowl and rub to a fine breadcrumb texture; blend in the sugar and ground hazelnuts. Press the mixture into a ball.

2. Divide the mixture in 2 and roll out each piece into a round 20 cm (8 inches) in diameter, patching as necessary. Place the rounds on greased and floured baking sheets and bake in a preheated oven for 10-15 minutes until lightly coloured, taking care that they do not scorch.

3. Remove and cut one round into 8 triangular pieces. Cool the pastries on a wire tray. **A**

4. To assemble, place the cooled pastry base on a serving plate and smooth or pipe the Cheese cream filling on top. Stand the pastry triangles on top in a fan arrangement, supported if necessary by raspberries. Arrange the rest of the raspberries on top. If liked, pipe with whipped cream. Serve within 1 hour.

A Hazelnut pastry can be prepared up to 3 weeks in advance if stored in an airtight tin, but once exposed to the air it softens in a few hours.

FROM THE LEFT Hazelnut and chocolate cheesecake; Chocolate truffle torte; Hazelnut cheese galette

LINDY'S CHEESECAKE

Serves 10-12
Pastry:
120 g (4½ oz) plain flour, sifted
120 g (4½ oz) butter, chilled and diced
40 g (1½ oz) caster sugar
1 teaspoon grated lemon zest
1 egg yolk
Filling:
1 kg (2 lb) curd cheese
350 g (12 oz) caster sugar
40 g (1½ oz) plain flour
2 tablespoons grated orange zest
1 tablespoon grated lemon zest
2 egg yolks
5 eggs
100 ml (3½ fl oz) double cream
To decorate:
candied orange peel
icing sugar

Preparation time: 45 minutes plus cooling
Cooking time: 1¾ hours
Oven: 200°C, 400°F, Gas Mark 6
then: 230°C, 450°F, Gas Mark 8
then: 110°C, 225°F, Gas Mark ¼

1. Prepare the pastry as for Shortcrust pastry (page 8)
2. Remove the sides of a 24 cm (9½ inch) springform tin and grease the base.
3. Roll out half the pastry and line the base. Prick all over with a fork and par-bake for 15 minutes until pale golden (page 8). Cool on a wire tray. Increase the oven temperature.
4. Roll out the remaining pastry to the same thickness as the base and cut out 2 strips, the depth of the tin, which will line the sides of the tin when laid end to end.
5. Grease the sides of the tin and snap them back on to the base. Arrange the pastry strips along the sides, pressing them lightly but firmly into the pastry base.
6. Beat the curd cheese with the sugar and flour. Beat in the orange and lemon zest and the egg yolks, one at a time. Beat in the eggs, then stir in the cream.
7. Pour the mixture into the case and bake in a preheated oven for 15 minutes, then reduce the oven temperature and bake for about 1¼ hours (test with a fine skewer after 1 hour). Cool in the tin on a wire tray. Ⓐ Ⓕ
8. To serve, carefully remove the sides of the tin and set the cake on a serving plate. Decorate with candied peel and icing sugar and serve with Apricot purée.

Ⓐ May be prepared up to 1 day ahead. Cover and chill until required.
Ⓕ May be frozen for up to 2 months. Defrost for 2 hours at room temperature.

APRICOT PURÉE

225 g (8 oz) apricot jam
50 g (2 oz) sugar
300 ml (½ pint) water
25 g (1 oz) cornflour
2 tablespoons water
3 tablespoons lemon juice or Kirsch
50 g (2 oz) nibbed almonds (optional)

Preparation time: 20 minutes
Cooking time: 10 minutes

1. Heat the jam, sugar and water in a small pan until dissolved, then boil for 5 minutes.
2. Draw off the heat and strain. Mix the cornflour with the water and stir in. Cook, stirring over a gentle heat until thickened.
3. Cool slightly, then mix in the lemon juice and nibbed almonds (if using). Chill.
4. Serve with the chilled cheesecake.

FROM THE LEFT Lindy's cheesecake served with Apricot purée; Fresh strawberry cake

FRESH STRAWBERRY CAKE

Serves 6

1 quantity Soured cream pastry (see Apricot cheesecake, page 16)

300 g (11 oz) strawberries, washed but not hulled

1 tablespoon caster sugar

150 ml (¼ pint) double cream, to decorate

Cheese cream filling:

250 g (9 oz) curd cheese

65 g (2½ oz) caster sugar

2 tablespoons soured cream

2 tablespoons Grand Marnier

150 ml (¼ pint) double cream

Preparation time: 50 minutes
Cooking time: 25-30 minutes
Oven: 200°C, 400°F, Gas Mark 6
then: 180°C, 350°F, Gas Mark 4

Here is a variation of strawberry shortcake.

1. Divide the pastry in 2 and roll out each piece into a round 20 cm (8 inches) in diameter. Place on baking sheets and bake for 10 minutes. Reduce oven temperature and bake for a further 15-20 minutes. **A**

2. Reserve 5 strawberries with stalks for decoration, hull the rest. Slice 50 g (2 oz), crush the rest, and combine, together with the tablespoon of sugar. **A**

3. For the filling, cream the curd cheese with the sugar, then blend in the soured cream and Grand Marnier. Whip the double cream and fold in. **A**

4. Place 1 pastry round on a serving plate and spread with half of the cheese cream filling. Spread the strawberry mixture on top and then cover with the remaining filling. Set the other pastry round on top. Chill.

5. To serve, spread or pipe whipped cream on top of the cake and decorate with the reserved strawberries.

A The pastry rounds, strawberry pulp and filling may be prepared up to 8 hours in advance; cover and keep chilled until ready to assemble the cake.

RUM, CREAM CHEESE AND LEMON TORTE

Serves 10-12
100 g (4 oz) sultanas
5 tablespoons dark rum
300 g (11 oz) curd cheese
75 g (3 oz) caster sugar
250 g (9 oz) lemon curd
4 teaspoons powdered gelatine dissolved in 3 tablespoons very hot water
350 ml (12 fl oz) double cream
2 tablespoons chopped pistachio nuts
Base:
2 tablespoons water
75 g (3 oz) sugar
1 Genoese sponge cake 24 cm (9½ inch) in diameter (page 11)
To decorate:
whipped cream
flaked toasted almonds
icing sugar

Preparation time: 30 minutes plus soaking and chilling
Cooking time: 2 minutes

1. Soak the sultanas in 2 tablespoons of rum for 30 minutes. Slice off the top of the Genoese sponge and reserve. Place the bottom piece in a 24 cm (9½ inch) springform tin.
2. Beat the curd cheese with the caster sugar and lemon curd. Stir in the dissolved gelatine and put to one side until on the point of setting.
3. Lightly whip the double cream and fold in with the soaked sultanas and chopped pistachios.
4. Put the water and sugar in a small pan. Heat gently until the sugar has dissolved then boil for 5 seconds. Allow to cool slightly then mix in the remaining rum.
5. Sprinkle the rum syrup over the cake layer in the tin. Pour in the filling.
6. Cut the remaining sponge layer into 12 triangular pieces. Arrange 10 of them evenly on top of the filling. Chill for 5-6 hours. Ⓐ
7. To serve, carefully remove the sides of the tin and set the torte on a serving plate. Pipe with whipped cream, scatter with flaked almonds and dredge with icing sugar.

Ⓐ May be prepared 1 day in advance. Cover and chill until required.

ROSE CHEESECAKE

Serves 8
1 quantity Soured cream pastry (see Apricot cheesecake, page 16)
120 g (4½ oz) butter, softened
500 g (1¼ lb) curd cheese
225 g (8 oz) caster sugar
4 eggs, separated
25 g (1 oz) candied orange peel, chopped
1 teaspoon grated lemon zest
1 teaspoon rosewater
1½ tablespoons ground almonds
150 g (5 oz) rose preserve
To decorate:
crystallized roses or crystallized rose petals
icing sugar

Preparation time: 35 minutes
Cooking time: 1 hour 15 minutes
Oven: 200°C, 400°F, Gas Mark 6
then: 180°C, 350°F, Gas Mark 4

The perfumed flower waters of rose and orange blossom have been used in Middle Eastern cooking for centuries. So too has a rose preserve, which is made from the crushed petals of the eglantine rose mixed with icing sugar. The jam is still very popular in Poland and is used as a filling in several Polish pastries, of which this is typical. Rose preserve can be bought in Middle Eastern and Greek food stores. If necessary redcurrant jelly can be used instead.

1. Roll out the pastry into a round 28 cm (11 inches) in diameter and line a 22 cm (8½ inch) springform tin so that the pastry covers the base and extends 2.5 cm (1 inch) up the sides. Par-bake (page 8) for 15 minutes. Cool in the tin on a wire tray. Turn down the oven temperature.
2. Meanwhile, cream the butter and beat in the curd cheese and sugar. Beat in the egg yolks, one at a time, then mix in the candied peel, lemon zest and rosewater.
3. Whisk the egg whites until stiff and fold them lightly into the mixture with the ground almonds.
4. Spread the rose preserve over the base of the pastry case. Pour in the cheese filling and bake in a preheated oven for 1 hour. Cool in the tin on a wire tray. Ⓐ
5. To serve, carefully remove the sides of the tin and set the cake on a serving plate. Decorate with crystallized roses and dredge with icing sugar.

Ⓐ May be prepared up to 2 days in advance. Cover and chill until required. Serve at room temperature.

CLOCKWISE FROM THE LEFT Rum, cream cheese and lemon torte; Rose cheesecake; Chocolate and ginger cheesecake

CHOCOLATE AND GINGER CHEESECAKE

100 g (4 oz) dark dessert chocolate, broken in pieces
225 g (8 oz) curd or cream cheese
100 g (4 oz) brown sugar
1 teaspoon ground ginger
pinch of salt
2 eggs, separated
2 teaspoons powdered gelatine, dissolved in 3 tablespoons very hot water
150 ml (¼ pint) whipping cream
75 g (3 oz) preserved ginger, chopped
1 Chocolate digestive crumb base in a 20 cm (8 inch) springform tin (page 7)

Preparation time: 45 minutes plus chilling
Cooking time: 5 minutes

This cheesecake has a rich chocolate base covered with crunchy ginger pieces which contrast deliciously with the rich smooth filling.

1. Melt the chocolate in a small heatproof bowl over a saucepan of simmering water. Cool.
2. Beat the cheese with 75 g (3 oz) of the sugar, the ginger, melted chocolate and salt. Beat in the egg yolks, one at a time, and then stir in the dissolved gelatine. Put the mixture to one side until almost on the point of setting.
3. Whip the egg whites until stiff then beat in the reserved brown sugar.
4. Whip the cream. Reserve 3 tablespoons for decoration, and fold the rest into the mixture with alternate spoonfuls of beaten egg white.
5. Reserve a few pieces of chopped ginger for decoration and sprinkle the remainder over the chocolate base. Pour in the filling and smooth over. Chill for 3-4 hours. Ⓐ Ⓕ
6. To serve, carefully remove the sides of the tin and set the cheesecake on a serving plate. Decorate with the reserved whipped cream and ginger pieces.

Ⓐ May be made 1-2 days in advance. Cover and chill until required. Decorate just before serving.
Ⓕ May be frozen for up to 1 month.

FROM THE LEFT Lemon japonais; Toasted almond torte; Cream cheese millefeuilles

LEMON JAPONAIS

Serves 10-12
Meringue:
2 egg whites
90 g (3½ oz) caster sugar
50 g (2 oz) ground toasted hazelnuts
1 tablespoon plain flour
75 g (3 oz) dark dessert chocolate, broken in pieces
Filling:
6 tablespoons lemon curd
3 tablespoons apricot jam
1 Fatless sponge cake 24 cm (9½ inches) in diameter
  (page 10)
2 tablespoons water
1 quantity Lemon cheesecake filling (see Chilled lemon
  cheesecake, page 25)
50 g (2 oz) toasted hazelnuts, chopped
To decorate:
chocolate curls
lemon slices

___

Preparation time: 1 hour plus cooling and chilling
Cooking time: 1 hour 20 minutes
Oven: 150°C, 300°F, Gas Mark 2

1. Line the base of a 24 cm (9½ inch) springform tin with non-stick silicone paper and lightly oil the sides.
2. Whisk the egg whites until stiff; sift in half the sugar and beat lightly until the mixture is satiny smooth. Sift over the remaining sugar and fold in. Fold in the ground hazelnuts and the flour. Spoon the mixture into the tin and smooth over. Bake for 1 hour.
3. Carefully remove from the tin and peel off the silicone paper. Cool on a wire tray.
4. Melt the chocolate in a small heatproof bowl over a saucepan of simmering water. Cool. Coat the meringue top with melted chocolate and leave to set.
5. Re-line the base of the tin with silicone paper and lightly oil the sides. Place the meringue in the tin, chocolate side down. Spread the lemon curd on top.
6. Gently heat the apricot jam with the water and stir to dissolve. Sieve, then use some to brush a thin layer over the sponge cake. Place the sponge cake, apricot glaze side up, in the tin.
7. Pour the lemon cheesecake filling into the tin and smooth over. Chill for 3-4 hours until set.
8. Carefully remove the sides of the tin and set the cake on a serving plate. Brush the sides of the sponge and the meringue layers with the remaining apricot glaze and press in the chopped hazelnuts.
9. Decorate with chocolate curls and lemon slices.

TOASTED ALMOND TORTE

Serves 12
65 g (2½ oz) strong plain flour, sifted
pinch of salt
1 teaspoon caster sugar
50 g (2 oz) salted butter, diced
120 ml (4 fl oz) water
2 eggs, lightly beaten
1 teaspoon brandy
100 g (4 oz) flaked almonds
1 Sweet shortcrust pastry base 26 cm (10½ inches) in
   diameter, baked blind (page 8)
3 egg yolks
50 g (2 oz) caster sugar
1 teaspoon grated lemon zest
250 g (8 oz) curd cheese
2 tablespoons Kirsch
1 tablespoon powdered gelatine dissolved in 2 tablespoons
   very hot water
300 ml (½ pint) double cream
2 tablespoons apricot jam
3 tablespoons cranberry jam
To decorate:
nectarine or peach slices
icing sugar

Preparation time: 1½ hours plus chilling
Cooking time: 40 minutes
Oven: 230°C, 450°F, Gas Mark 8

1. Sift the flour with the salt and sugar. Place the butter and water in a saucepan and heat gently until the butter has melted, then raise the heat and bring to a rolling boil. Draw off the heat and immediately tip in the flour. Beat briskly over a low heat until it forms a ball that rolls cleanly around the pan. Cool for 5 minutes.
2. Beat in the beaten eggs, a little at a time, until the mixture is firm, shiny and elastic. Beat in the brandy.
3. Draw 3 circles, 22 cm (8½ inches) in diameter, on sheets of silicone paper on baking sheets. Spread the choux pastry over the three circles.
4. Scatter the flaked almonds over each circle and bake in a preheated oven for 10 minutes. Cool.
5. Beat the egg yolks with the sugar and zest until doubled in bulk. Beat in the cheese and Kirsch. Fold in the gelatine and leave until on the point of setting.
6. Lightly whip the double cream and fold in.
7. Gently heat the apricot jam until liquid. Strain and brush over the cooked shortcrust base.
8. To assemble the torte, lay a choux pastry layer on top of the shortcrust base. Spread with half of the filling. Spread the second layer with cranberry jam and place on top of the filling. Spread the remaining filling over and top with the last choux layer.
9. Arrange the nectarine slices around the rim of the base, dust with icing sugar and serve.

CREAM CHEESE MILLEFEUILLES

Serves 10
375 g (13 oz) puff pastry
300 ml (½ pint) milk
piece of vanilla pod 2.5 cm (1 inch) long, split
6 egg yolks
175 g (6 oz) icing sugar, sifted
pinch of salt
1 tablespoon powdered gelatine dissolved in 2 tablespoons
   very hot water
450 g (1 lb) curd cheese
300 ml (½ pint) double cream
75 g (3 oz) candied orange and lemon peel, chopped
4 tablespoons apricot jam
icing sugar, to decorate

Preparation time: 50 minutes plus chilling
Cooking time: 35 minutes
Oven: 220°C, 425°F, Gas Mark 7

This cheesecake dessert is best eaten the day it is made, as puff pastry deteriorates rapidly.

1. Divide the pastry in two and roll out each piece fractionally larger than the base of a 25 cm (10 inch) springform tin. Trim each piece to fit the base exactly with a sharp knife that has been dipped in boiling water, leaving a very clean edge.
2. Run ice-cold water over 2 baking sheets until chilled, and leave wet. Place a pastry round on each tray, prick each round all over with a fork and chill for 30 minutes.
3. Bake the pastry rounds in a preheated oven for 20 minutes until brown and well puffed. Remove and, while still hot, cut 1 round into 10 triangular pieces. Cool on a wire tray.
4. Line the base of a 25 cm (10 inch) springform tin with non-stick silicone paper.
5. Scald the milk with the vanilla pod then leave to infuse until the milk has cooled slightly. Remove the vanilla pod.
6. Beat the egg yolks with the icing sugar. Blend in the warm vanilla milk and stir over a gentle heat until the custard has thickened. Take off the heat, add the salt and stir in the dissolved gelatine. Put to one side until the mixture has cooled and is on the point of setting.
7. Mix in the curd cheese. Lightly whip the double cream and fold in with the chopped peel.
8. Place the whole pastry base in the prepared cake tin. In a small pan, heat the apricot jam until liquid. Strain, then brush over the pastry base in the tin. Pour the cheese filling into the tin and stand the pastry triangles on top in a fan arrangement. Chill for 3-4 hours.
9. To serve, carefully remove the sides of the tin, set the cake on a serving plate and dust with icing sugar.

EXOTIC CHEESECAKES

MOCHA AND CHESTNUT CHEESECAKE ROULADE

Serves 6
½ quantity Chocolate fatless sponge cake mixture
  (page 10)
2 tablespoons caster sugar (for dredging)
Filling:
2 teaspoons instant coffee powder
1 teaspoon boiling water
275 g (10 oz) curd cheese
40 g (1½ oz) caster sugar
2 tablespoons Tia Maria
120 g (4½ oz) unsweetened chestnut purée
120 ml (4½ fl oz) double cream
To decorate:
Chocolate rounds (see opposite)
marrons glacés (optional)

Preparation time: 30 minutes plus chilling
Cooking time: 8-10 minutes
Oven: 230°C, 450°F, Gas Mark 8

1. Line a 25 × 36 cm (10 × 14 inches) Swiss roll tin with non-stick silicone paper, leaving a 5 cm (2 inch) overlap all around. Grease with butter.
2. Pour the chocolate sponge mixture into the tin and smooth over. Bake in a preheated oven for 8-10 minutes until well risen.
3. Meanwhile, lay a large sheet of non-stick silicone paper on a work top and dredge with the caster sugar. When the sponge is cooked, turn it out on to the paper, peel off the lining paper and trim off the crisp edges with a sharp knife.
4. Lay another sheet of silicone paper on top and roll up the sponge from the short side. Leave to cool on a wire tray.
5. Make the filling by hand. Dissolve the coffee powder in the boiling water and leave to cool. Beat together the curd cheese, sugar, cooled coffee liquid and Tia Maria. Beat in the chestnut purée. Lightly whip the double cream and fold in.
6. Unroll the sponge and spread over two-thirds of the filling to within 1 cm (½ inch) of the edges.
7. Roll up the filled sponge from the short edge and trim the ends neatly. Transfer, seam side down, to a serving plate.
8. Smooth or pipe the remaining filling on top and decorate with Chocolate rounds and marrons glacés (if using). Chill well before serving.

CHOCOLATE ROUNDS

1. Melt 50 g (2 oz) dark dessert chocolate in a heatproof bowl set over a pan of hot water. Spread the melted chocolate to a thickness of 2 mm (1/10 inch) on non-stick silicone paper or tinfoil.
2. When it has just started to harden, stamp out circles with a small metal pastry cutter. Leave to cool.
3. Gently lift the discs from the paper with a spatula and store in an airtight container, between sheets of silicone paper, until ready for use.

CHEESECAKE ALASKA

Serves 8
1 quantity Pistachio filling (see Pistachio diplomat, page 57)
3 egg whites
150 g (5 oz) caster sugar
Sweet shortcrust pastry for a 26 cm (10½ inch) tin, rolled out into a rectangle 4 cm (1½ inches) larger all round than the loaf tin, baked blind (page 8)
2 tablespoons chopped pistachio nuts

Preparation time: 45 minutes plus freezing and thawing
Cooking time: 5 minutes
Oven: 230°C, 450°F, Gas Mark 8

1. Pour the pistachio filling into a 450 g (1 lb) loaf tin and freeze. **F**
2. Transfer to the refrigerator and leave for 30 minutes to soften slightly.
3. Whisk the egg whites until they hold firm snowy peaks. Whisk in 50 g (2 oz) of the sugar and beat with a handheld beater until the mixture is smooth and glossy. Fold in the remaining sugar by hand.
4. Place the frozen filling on the centre of the short-crust base. Cover completely with meringue, swirled with a palette knife or piped with a large star nozzle. Make sure that the covering is completely air-tight.
5. Bake in the hot oven for 5 minutes until light brown. Scatter the chopped pistachios over and serve immediately.

F The pistachio filling may be frozen for up to 2 months.

FROM THE BOTTOM Mocha and chestnut cheesecake roulade; Cheesecake Alaska

RASPBERRY BAGATELLE

Serves 10

1 Genoese sponge cake 24 cm (9½ inches) in diameter (page 11)
75 g (3 oz) granulated sugar
2 tablespoons water
6 tablespoons framboise liqueur
450 g (1 lb) curd cheese
120 g (4½ oz) caster sugar
4 eggs, separated
100 ml (3½ fl oz) double cream
2 tablespoons powdered gelatine dissolved in 5 tablespoons very hot water
450 g (1 lb) raspberries, defrosted if frozen

To decorate:
icing sugar
scented geranium or lemon balm leaves

Preparation time: 1 hour plus chilling overnight
Cooking time: 5 minutes

This makes a pretty dessert for a summer party.

1. Line the base and sides of a 24 cm (9½ inch) springform tin with non-stick silicone paper.
2. Cut the sponge in 2 horizontally and drop one half into the prepared tin.
3. Put the granulated sugar and water in a small pan and heat gently until dissolved, then boil for 10 seconds. Cool slightly then stir in 3 tablespoons of the liqueur. Brush the base in the tin with syrup.
4. Cream the curd cheese and caster sugar. Beat in the egg yolks, then the cream and remaining liqueur.
5. Whip the egg whites until stiff. Slowly beat the dissolved gelatine into the filling mixture and immediately fold in the beaten egg white.
6. Spread a little filling over the base in the tin.
7. Set aside a few raspberries for decoration. Arrange a row of the remaining raspberries around the edge of the base, and arrange the rest in the centre.
8. Pour the rest of the filling over the fruit. Lay the second sponge layer on top and brush with the remaining syrup. Chill overnight.
9. Set the cake on a serving plate and sift a layer of icing sugar over the top. Decorate with the reserved raspberries and geranium leaves.

SUMMER PUDDING CHEESECAKE

Serves 6

1 × 400 g (14 oz) crusty white loaf, crusts removed and cut into 7-8 slices

Filling:

225 g (8 oz) fresh redcurrants, stalks removed

350 g (12 oz) black cherries, stoned

225 g (8 oz) fresh raspberries

150 ml (¼ pint) water

100 g (4 oz) sugar

Topping:

75 ml (3 fl oz) double cream

100 g (4 oz) curd or cream cheese

1½ teaspoons grated lemon zest

1½ tablespoons Kirsch

40 g (1½ oz) caster sugar

To decorate:

1 egg white

2 tablespoons caster sugar

6-10 redcurrants with stalks

Preparation time: 45 minutes plus chilling overnight
Cooking time: 10 minutes

1. Closely line the sides and the base of an oiled 450 g (1 lb) loaf tin with the bread, trimming where necessary, reserving 3 slices for the top.

2. Place the redcurrants, cherries and raspberries in a saucepan with the water and sugar. Bring to the boil, then simmer gently until the sugar had dissolved. Strain the fruit through a nylon sieve, reserving the juice, and set aside to cool.

3. Brush the bread pieces with the reserved juices, making sure that they are well soaked.

4. Fill the loaf tin with the fruit and cover closely with the remaining bread slices. Brush with more of the reserved juice (there will be some left over).

5. Lay a double sheet of tinfoil on top of the mould and weigh down. Chill overnight. **F**

6. Make the topping by hand. Lightly whip the double cream and gently fold into the cheese. Fold in the lemon zest, Kirsch and caster sugar.

7. Unmould the summer pudding on to a serving plate and smooth the topping over the top and sides to cover completely. Chill.

8. Meanwhile, lightly beat the egg white for decoration and dip the redcurrants with stalks into it. Roll them in the caster sugar.

9. Arrange the redcurrants on top of the cheesecake and serve.

F May be frozen for up to 1 month. Defrost at room temperature for 2-3 hours before decorating.

Variation:

A 'winter' Summer pudding can be made by substituting the following filling ingredients for those in the main recipe.

350 g (12 oz) cranberries

450 g (1 lb) frozen raspberries, defrosted, juice reserved

3 long strips orange peel

300 ml (10 fl oz) water

200 g (7 oz) sugar

2 tablespoons grated orange zest

1. Place the cranberries in a saucepan with the reserved raspberry juice, orange peel and water. Bring to the boil and simmer for 3-4 minutes until the berries start to pop. Stir in the raspberries.

2. Draw off the heat and stir in the sugar and orange zest.

3. Strain the fruit through the nylon sieve and remove the strips of peel, reserving the juice. Leave to cool and proceed as for the main recipe.

FROM THE LEFT Raspberry bagatelle; Summer pudding cheesecake

PISTACHIO DIPLOMAT

Serves 8
26 boudoir sponge biscuits
Pistachio filling:
225 g (8 oz) cream cheese
65 g (2½ oz) icing sugar, sifted
3 tablespoons Cointreau
300 ml (½ pint) soured cream
150 ml (¼ pint) double cream
90 g (3½ oz) pistachio nuts or hazelnuts, chopped
To decorate:
whipped cream
lemon peel curls
ribbon (optional)

Preparation time: 15-20 minutes plus freezing and chilling

1. Line the base and sides of a 450 g (1 lb) loaf tin with non-stick silicone paper. Arrange 22 boudoir biscuits, upright, around the edge of the tin.
2. Cream the cream cheese with the icing sugar then blend in the Cointreau.
3. Whip the soured cream and the double cream separately until stiff. Fold the creams into the mixture with the chopped pistachios.
4. Carefully pour the mixture into the tin and trim the tops of the biscuits. Lay the remaining boudoir biscuits on top. Freeze for at least 8 hours. **F**
5. One hour before serving unmould on to a serving plate and remove the silicone paper.
6. Decorate with rosettes of whipped cream and lemon peel curls. Tie the ribbon around the centre of the diplomat, if using, and chill for 30 minutes before serving.

F May be frozen for up to 2 months.

STRAWBERRY CHEESECAKE PANCAKES

Serves 6
300 g (11 oz) curd cheese
3 eggs, separated
150 g (5 oz) caster sugar
2 tablespoons cornflour
1 tablespoon grated orange zest
2 tablespoons Cointreau
450 g (1 lb) fresh strawberries, hulled and sliced
12 Dessert pancakes (page 11)
fresh strawberries, to decorate

**Preparation time: 30 minutes
Cooking time: 10-15 minutes
Oven: 220°C, 425°F, Gas Mark 7**

PEACH CHEESECAKE

Serves 14
50 g (2 oz) ground almonds
1 Sweet shortcrust pastry base in a 26 cm (10½ inch) springform tin, baked blind (page 8)
750 g (1½ lb) fresh peaches, halved, stoned and sliced, or 1 × 800 g (1 lb 12 oz) can sliced white peaches, drained
400 g (14 oz) curd cheese
100 g (4 oz) caster sugar
1 teaspoon grated lemon zest
1 teaspoon lemon juice
120 ml (4 fl oz) soured cream
4 eggs, separated
icing sugar, to decorate

**Preparation time: 40 minutes
Cooking time: 1 hour 20 minutes
Oven: 160°C, 325°F, Gas Mark 3**

1. Sprinkle the ground almonds evenly over the pastry base in the tin and press down lightly.
2. Arrange the sliced peaches on the almond base, packing them tightly together.
3. Beat together the curd cheese, sugar, lemon zest and lemon juice. Blend in the soured cream and egg yolks.
4. Whip the egg whites until stiff and gently fold them into the mixture.
5. Pour the filling into the tin and smooth over.
6. Bake in a preheated oven for 1 hour 20 minutes until well risen and golden. Leave to cool in the tin for 15 minutes before removing the sides of the tin and transferring the cake to a wire tray to cool. **F**
7. Dredge with icing sugar to serve.

F May be frozen for up to 2 months. Defrost at room temperature for 1 hour.

1. Beat the curd cheese with the egg yolks, sugar and cornflour. Stir in the orange zest and Cointreau. Whip the egg whites until stiff and fold them in.
2. Spoon a little cheese mixture on to each pancake and lay some sliced strawberries on top, dividing the cheese mixture and filling equally between the pancakes. Roll up the pancakes.
3. Lay the pancakes in a greased ovenproof dish and place in a preheated oven for 10-15 minutes until warmed through.
4. Serve hot, decorated with fresh strawberries and accompanied by pouring cream.

FROM THE LEFT Pistachio diplomat; Strawberry cheesecake pancakes

TOPFEN TORTE

Serves 14
Sweet shortcrust pastry for a 26 cm (10½ inch) springform
    tin (page 8)
Filling 1:
75 g (3 oz) butter, softened
3 eggs, separated
75 g (3 oz) caster sugar
1 tablespoon vanilla sugar
350 g (12 oz) curd cheese
Filling 2:
6 eggs, separated
100 g (4 oz) butter, melted
100 g (4 oz) caster sugar
65 g (2½ oz) plain flour, sifted
To decorate:
icing sugar
1 flower with a leaf, or a few crystallized rose petals

Preparation time: 50 minutes
Cooking time: 1 hour 20 minutes
Oven: 180°C, 350°F, Gas Mark 4

1. Prepare the pastry case in 2 sections as for Lindy's
cheesecake, page 46.
2. To make Filling 1, beat the butter with the egg yolks
until pale and creamy. Beat in the caster sugar, vanilla
sugar and curd cheese.
3. Whip the egg whites until stiff and fold them into
the mixture. Pour the mixture into the pastry case in
the tin and smooth over.
4. To make Filling 2, whip the egg whites until stiff.
Lightly whisk the egg yolks and fold them into the
beaten egg white, a small amount at a time, with a
large metal spoon.
5. Fold in a third of the butter and then a third of the
sugar. Continue until all the butter and sugar have
been added. Sift the flour over and fold in.
6. Pour the second filling into the tin on top of the first
and gently smooth over
7. Bake in the preheated oven for 1 hour until puffed
and golden. Cool in the tin on a wire tray. F
8 To serve, dredge with icing sugar and place the
flower in the centre.

F May be frozen for up to 2 months. Defrost at room
temperature for 1-2 hours, decorate and serve.

BOREKIAS

Makes 20
Filling:
450 g (1 lb) curd cheese
4 tablespoons honey
2 tablespoons caster sugar
1 teaspoon ground cinnamon
Pastry:
450 g (1 lb) filo pastry (see page 73)
225 g (8 oz) unsalted butter, melted
Syrup:
350 ml (12 fl oz) honey
250 ml (8 fl oz) water
1 tablespoon orange-flower water

Preparation time: 1 hour
Cooking time: 1 hour
Oven: 160°C, 325°F, Gas Mark 3
then: 230°C, 450°F, Gas Mark 8

These classic Middle Eastern pastries are modern-day
relatives of the original cheesecakes. Orange-flower
water may be found in chemist shops and good
delicatessens.

1. Beat together the cheese, honey, sugar and
cinnamon.
2. Brush a 24 cm (9½ inch) square baking tin with
melted butter.
3. Unwrap the filo pastry and divide in half. Wrap one
half to prevent it drying out whilst you work with the
other.
4. Lay one filo pastry sheet in the tin, brush the top
with melted butter and fold in the edges for an exact fit.
Lay the remaining sheets of filo in the tin in the same
way.
5. Spread the filling over the filo pastry in the tin.
6. Unwrap the remaining sheets of filo pastry and lay
them on top of the filling, brushing each one with
melted butter as before. Brush the top with melted
butter.
7. With a sharp knife cut lengthwise lines in the
pastry and cut across these diagonally to make
diamond shapes.
8. Place in a preheated oven and bake for 30 minutes,
then raise the oven temperature and bake for a further
15 minutes until puffed and golden.
9. Meanwhile make the syrup. Put the honey and
water in a pan and stir over a gentle heat until the
honey has dissolved, then simmer steadily until the
syrup is thick enough to coat the back of a wooden
spoon. Stir in the orange-flower water. Chill.
10. When the borekias are ready, remove from the
oven and immediately pour the hot syrup over. Leave to
cool in the tin.
11. Cut into portions and serve.

BRANDY SNAPS

Makes 24
120 g (4½ oz) plain flour
¼ teaspoon ground ginger
¼ teaspoon ground allspice
100 g (4 oz) butter, chilled and cubed
100 g (4 oz) caster sugar
120 ml (4 fl oz) golden syrup
1 teaspoon brandy
175 ml (6 fl oz) double cream
65 g (2½ oz) caster sugar
225 g (8 oz) curd cheese
1 tablespoon grated lemon zest
1 teaspoon ground ginger
50 g (2 oz) chopped mixed peel
chopped candied orange peel, to decorate

Preparation time: 35 minutes
Cooking time: about 1 hour
Oven: 170°C, 325°F, Gas Mark 3

FROM THE RIGHT Brandy snaps; Borekias

1. Sift the flour with the ginger and allspice. Drop in the cubed butter and rub to a fine breadcrumb texture. Stir in the sugar. Add the golden syrup and brandy and knead to a fine elastic dough.
2. Pinch off pieces of dough the size of an unshelled walnut and roll into balls. Place 3 balls 12 cm (5 inches) apart on a greased baking sheet and flatten slightly.
3. Bake in the preheated oven for 7 minutes. Remove and leave to cool for a minute or two, and then roll each piece around the greased handle of a wooden spoon to make a traditional brandy snap shape.
4. Draw each snap off the spoon as soon as it is set and leave to cool on a wire tray. Prepare 21 more brandy snaps in the same way.
5. To make the filling, lightly whip the cream and beat in the sugar. Gently fold the sweetened cream into the curd cheese, 2 tablespoons at a time. Fold in the lemon zest, ginger and chopped mixed peel.
6. Fill a piping bag fitted with a large star nozzle with the filling and fill the brandy snaps from both ends. Stud the cream with candied orange peel and serve.

CHOCOLATE AND ORANGE ROLL

Serves 6
½ quantity Fatless sponge cake mixture (page 10)
2 tablespoons caster sugar, for dredging
Grand Marnier filling:
175 ml (6 fl oz) double cream
225 g (8 oz) curd or cream cheese
1 tablespoon grated lemon zest
3 tablespoons Grand Marnier
50 g (2 oz) candied orange peel, chopped
65 g (2½ oz) caster sugar
To decorate:
100 g (4 oz) dark dessert chocolate, broken in pieces
candied orange peel
toasted flaked almonds

Preparation time: 25 minutes plus chilling
Cooking time: 8-10 minutes
Oven: 230°C, 450°F, Gas Mark 8

If simpler, prepare the full quantity of sponge mixture and bake in two parts. Freeze one half unfilled.

1. Line a 25 × 36 cm (10 × 14 inch) Swiss roll tin with non-stick silicone paper, leaving a 5 cm (2 inch) overlap all around. Grease with butter.
2. Pour the sponge cake mixture into the tin and smooth over. Bake in a preheated oven for 8-10 minutes until well risen and golden.
3. Meanwhile lay a large sheet of non-stick silicone paper on a work top and dredge with the caster sugar. When the sponge is cooked, turn it out on to the paper, peel off the lining paper, and trim off the crisp edges with a sharp knife.
4. Lay another sheet of silicone paper on top and roll the sponge up from the short side. Leave to cool on a wire tray.
5. Make the filling by hand. Lightly whip the double cream and gently fold into the cheese. Fold in the lemon zest, Grand Marnier, candied peel and caster sugar.
6. Unroll the sponge and spread the filling over to within 1 cm (½ inch) of the edge.
7. Roll up the filled sponge from the short edge and trim the ends neatly. Transfer, seam side down, to a serving plate.
8. Place the chocolate in a heatproof bowl over a saucepan of hot water and stir until melted. Pour the warm melted chocolate over the roll and smooth over with a palette knife that has been dipped in hot water.
9. Decorate with candied orange peel and toasted flaked almonds and serve. A

A May be prepared 5-6 hours in advance. Cover and keep chilled until required.

CHILLED APRICOT VACHERIN

Serves 10
3 tablespoons redcurrant or cranberry jelly
1 cooked Meringue base 24 cm (9½ inches) in diameter (see Lemon japonais, page 50)
1 × 800 g (1 lb 13 oz) can apricot halves, drained
1 quantity Grand Marnier filling (see Chocolate and orange roll, left)
chopped pistachio nuts, to decorate

Preparation time: 15 minutes plus chilling

1. Spread the jelly over the meringue base. Reserve 4 apricot halves for decoration, arrange the remainder over the meringue base.
2. Carefully spread the Grand Marnier filling over the apricots.
3. Decorate with chopped pistachios and the reserved apricots.
4. Chill for 1 hour before serving.

FROM THE LEFT Chilled apricot vacherin; Cheesecake chocolate brownies; Chocolate and orange roll

CHEESECAKE CHOCOLATE BROWNIES

Makes 16
Filling 1:
100 g (4 oz) cream cheese
25 g (1 oz) butter, softened
50 g (2 oz) caster sugar
1 tablespoon vanilla sugar
1 egg
25 g (1 oz) plain flour
Filling 2:
100 g (4 oz) dark dessert chocolate, broken in pieces
40 g (1½ oz) unsalted butter
2 eggs
150 g (5 oz) caster sugar
2 tablespoons plain flour
½ teaspoon baking powder
pinch of salt
2 drops bitter almond essence
150 g (5 oz) pecan nuts or toasted hazelnuts, chopped

Preparation time: 40 minutes
Cooking time: 40-45 minutes
Oven: 180°C, 350°F, Gas Mark 4

1. To make Filling 1, thoroughly cream the cheese and the butter. Beat in the caster sugar, vanilla sugar, egg and flour. Set aside.
2. To make Filling 2, melt the chocolate and butter in a heatproof bowl over simmering water. Stir until well blended then remove the bowl and allow to cool.
3. Lightly whisk the eggs and gradually beat in the sugar until the mixture is creamy and thick. Sift the flour with the baking powder and salt, and stir it into the mixture.
4. Stir the almond essence and 100 g (4 oz) of the chopped nuts into Filling 2.
5. Spread half of the second filling over the base of a 20 cm (8 inch) square baking tin. Spread Filling 1 on top, then top with the remaining portion of Filling 2.
6. Draw a knife through the mixture with a zigzag motion to produce a marbled effect and scatter the remaining chopped nuts on top.
7. Bake in the preheated oven for 35-40 minutes until almost dry and firm to the touch.
8. Cut into 16 squares whilst still warm. Leave to cool, in the tin, on a wire tray. Ⓐ

Ⓐ Can be prepared up to 5 days in advance. Store in an airtight tin until required.

TÚRÓTORTA

Serves 10

65 g (2½ oz) butter, diced
120 g (4½ oz) plain flour, sifted
1 teaspoon caster sugar
1 egg yolk
150 ml (¼ pint) soured cream
225 g (8 oz) curd cheese
6 eggs, separated
200 g (7 oz) caster sugar
1 tablespoon grated orange zest
1 tablespoon vanilla sugar or ½ teaspoon vanilla essence
icing sugar, to decorate

Preparation time: 40 minutes
Cooking time: 1 hour
Oven: 160°C, 325°F, Gas Mark 3

This Hungarian cheesecake will puff right up out of the tin as it cooks, but as it cools it shrinks, and you can gently push it back into place. The irregular surface is part of its charm.

1. Rub the butter into the flour. Add the sugar, egg yolk and soured cream and blend to a smooth, firm pastry.

2. Divide the dough in 3. Roll out each portion to fit the base of a 24 cm (9½ inch) springform tin. Grease the base of the tin and place 1 pastry round on it. Snap on the greased sides of the tin.

3. Cream the curd cheese then beat in the egg yolks, one at a time, the caster sugar, orange zest and vanilla sugar.

4. Whip the egg whites until stiff then fold them into the mixture.

5. Pour half the filling into the tin and lay a pastry round on top. Cover this with the rest of the filling and top with the remaining pastry round. Press down lightly with the hand to flatten.

6. Bake in the preheated oven for 1 hour until well risen. Cool in the tin on a wire tray.

7. Carefully remove the sides of the tin, dredge with icing sugar and serve.

RUSSIAN PASKHA

Serves 15
225 g (8 oz) unsalted butter, softened
175 g (6 oz) caster sugar
2 eggs
500 g (1¼ lb) curd cheese, which has been left overnight
  in a sieve, weighted, to drain
120 ml (4 fl oz) double cream
100 g (4 oz) toasted almonds, chopped
2 tablespoons pistachio nuts, chopped
100 g (4 oz) raisins
50 g (2 oz) candied orange and lemon peel, chopped
3 drops vanilla essence or ½ teaspoon rosewater
To decorate:
toasted almonds
halved glacé cherries
angelica strips

Preparation time: 30 minutes plus draining and chilling

This traditional Easter dessert is usually set in a pyramid-shaped wooden mould which has the imprint of the Russian Orthodox cross on one of its faces, but a well scrubbed clay flower pot, 15 cm (6 inches) wide and 14 cm (5½ inches) deep, can be used instead. Line it with muslin or cheesecloth as follows: place a large sheet of muslin or cheesecloth over the pot and cut a slit from one edge to the centre. Push the muslin into the pot, overlapping the cut edges, and smooth it against the sides. Make sure that the piece is large enough to leave an edge which can be folded over the top of the filled flowerpot. This cheesecake is very rich and should be served in small portions.

1. Beat the butter and sugar until pale and creamy; beat in the eggs one at a time.
2. Sieve in the drained curd cheese and beat well. Blend in the double cream.
3. Mix in the chopped almonds, pistachios, raisins, candied peel and vanilla essence.
4. Pour the mixture into the lined mould and fold over the edges of the muslin to cover the filling. Lay a small plate or saucer holding a 1 kg (2 lb) weight on top.
5. Place in the refrigerator and set a plate underneath to catch any moisture that drains out. Chill for 8-10 hours.
6. Unmould and peel off the muslin. Decorate with almonds, glacé cherries and angelica and serve.

POLISH CHEESECAKE

Serves 8
1 Sweet shortcrust pastry case 24 cm (9½ inches) in
  diameter, baked blind (page 8)
2 teaspoons grated lemon zest
1 tablespoon dark rum
1 tablespoon white wine
pinch of saffron strands
50 g (2 oz) raisins
75 g (3 oz) granulated sugar
2 tablespoons cold water
75 g (3 oz) ground almonds
5 egg yolks
450 g (1 lb) curd cheese
100 g (3½ oz) caster sugar
2 tablespoons flaked almonds
icing sugar, to serve

Preparation time: 45 minutes plus marinating
Cooking time: 1 hour
Oven: 200°C, 400°F, Gas Mark 6

Saffron has a very distinctive flavour and gives a rich golden tint to this cheesecake.

1. Combine the lemon zest and rum in one cup, combine the white wine and saffron in another cup; leave both mixtures to infuse for 2 hours.
2. Mix the two liquids together and pour over the raisins.
3. Put the granulated sugar and water in a small heavy-bottomed pan. Heat over a low flame until the sugar has dissolved, then boil to the thread stage (107°C, 225°F, or when a small amount dropped from a teaspoon on to a saucer forms a fine thread as it falls) this should take about 20 seconds. Draw off the heat and quickly stir in the ground almonds. Return to the heat and stir until the mixture has thickened.
4. Spread the warm mixture on the cooked pastry shell.
5. Beat the egg yolks, one at a time, into the curd cheese. Add the caster sugar and combine well. Beat in the soaked raisins and their marinade thoroughly.
6. Spread the cheese filling evenly over the first filling, scatter the almond flakes over and bake in the pre-heated oven for 1 hour until puffed and deep golden.
7. Cool on a wire tray. Dredge with icing sugar to serve.

FROM THE LEFT Túrótorta; Russian paskha

SAVOURY CHEESECAKES

FRESH VEGETABLE AND CHEESE TERRINE

Serves 12
400 g (14 oz) curd cheese, sieved and chilled
150 ml (¼ pint) soured cream, chilled
3 egg yolks
½ teaspoon salt
½ teaspoon freshly ground pepper
75 g (3 oz) watercress, washed and trimmed
1 quantity Savoury breadcrumb base (see Avocado and prawn cheesecake, page 75)
175 g (6 oz) baby carrots, peeled
175 g (6 oz) petit pois peas, fresh or frozen
200 g (7 oz) small courgettes
100 g (4 oz) small French beans, stringed, topped and tailed
1 lemon, peel and pith removed, thinly sliced

Preparation time: 1½ hours plus cooling and chilling overnight
Cooking time: 45 minutes
Oven: 180°C, 3500°F, Gas Mark 4

Here is a spectacular hors d'oeuvre for a special dinner party. The subtle flavour of the smooth cheese and watercress filling compliments the tiny crisp vegetables particularly well.

1. To make the stuffing, put the curd cheese in a large mixing bowl and gently stir in the soured cream and egg yolks. Add the salt and pepper and set aside.
2. Finely chop the watercress in a liquidizer or food processor and combine it with one third of the stuffing mixture. Chill both mixtures for 30 minutes.
3. Boil the carrots, peas, courgettes and beans in water separately for a very short time, making sure that they remain a little crisp. Drain and refresh with cold water. Cool.
4. Cut the courgettes in quarters lengthways.
5. Lightly oil a 22 × 12 cm (12 × 4 inch) terrine or a 1 kg (2 lb) loaf tin and, if metal, line with non-stick silicone paper. Arrange the lemon slices over the base.
6. Spread one third of the stuffing mixture without watercress in the bottom of the terrine. Arrange a row of courgettes, lengthwise, on top. Spread another third of the same stuffing mixture on top and then cover with a layer of peas. Spread over the remaining plain stuffing and arrange the beans lengthwise on top.
7. Spread over half the watercress stuffing, then arrange the carrots, lengthwise, on top. Spread the remaining watercress stuffing on top.
8. Cover with the herb breadcrumb base and press down gently.
9. Place the lid on the terrine, or cover tightly with tin foil.
10. Stand in a roasting pan filled with boiling water and cook in a preheated oven for 45 minutes, by which time the top should be starting to crack.
11. Remove and allow to cool, then chill overnight. Turn out on to a large serving plate and garnish with fresh chervil. Serve in slices with Chilled tomato sauce.

CHILLED TOMATO SAUCE

2 × 800 g (1 lb 13 oz) cans tomatoes, drained
1 teaspoon sugar
1 tablespoon tomato purée
2 tablespoons white wine vinegar
6 tablespoons olive oil
1 teaspoon salt
½ teaspoon freshly ground black pepper
1 tablespoon chopped tarragon or 3 teaspoons dried

Preparation time: 15 minutes

1. Liquidize the tomatoes in a food processor or blender and sieve. Chill the pulp.
2. Place the tomato pulp in a liquidizer bowl or blender goblet and add the sugar, tomato purée, vinegar and oil, drop by drop, whilst the blade is spinning. Blend well until smooth and thick.
3. Season with salt and pepper.
4. Stir in the chopped herbs and chill until ready to serve with the terrine.

Fresh vegetable and cheese terrine with Chilled tomato sauce

FROM THE TOP Talmouses with Brie; Pâte de fromage de chèvre

PÂTE DE FROMAGE DE CHÈVRE
Fresh Goat's Cheese Flan

Serves 8

2 tablespoons butter
2 tablespoons plain flour
250 ml (8 fl oz) milk
½ teaspoon freshly ground black pepper
2 egg yolks
200 g (7 oz) chèvre cheese, crumbled
25 g (1 oz) Parmesan cheese, grated
50 g (2 oz) cooked ham, finely chopped (optional)
1 Savoury shortcrust case in a 22 cm (8 inch) flan tin,
   par-baked (page 8)
fresh coriander to garnish

Preparation time: 25 minutes
Cooking time: 45 minutes
Oven: 190°C, 375°F, Gas Mark 5

1. Melt the butter in a pan, blend in the flour and cook over a low heat for 2-3 minutes, stirring constantly. Gradually pour on the milk, beating continuously.
2. Simmer the mixture gently, stirring, for 5 minutes, then mix in the pepper and egg yolks.
3. Draw the pan off the heat and add the cheeses. Return to the heat and stir until the mixture is well blended. Stir in the chopped ham (if using).
4. Pour the filling into the pastry case and bake in a preheated oven for 30 minutes until golden.
5. Serve the flan warm or cold, garnished with coriander leaves.

TALMOUSES WITH BRIE

Makes about 30
250 g (9 oz) puff pastry
120 ml (4 fl oz) milk
50 g (2 oz) butter, diced
pinch of salt
50 g (2 oz) plain flour
1 egg
1 egg yolk
100 g (4 oz) Brie cheese, rinded and mashed
1 tablespoon double cream
1 egg, lightly beaten, to glaze

Preparation time: 40 minutes
Cooking time: 40 minutes
Oven: 190°C, 375°F, Gas Mark 5

These flower-like pastries are made of a delicious light combination of puff pastry and Brie choux pastry.

1. Roll out the pastry 2 mm (1/16 inch) thick and with a very sharp knife cut into 30 pieces, 7½ cm (3 inch) square.
2. Gently heat the milk with the butter and salt. When the liquid is just boiling draw the pan off the heat and quickly tip in all the flour, combine and beat briskly over a low heat for a few seconds until the mixture forms a firm paste which rolls cleanly off the sides of the pan into a smooth ball. Leave to cool for 5 minutes.
3. Beat in the egg and egg yolk, one at a time, then blend in the cheese and cream.
4. Place a teaspoonful of the mixture in the centre of each pastry square. Moisten the 4 corners of each square with water, lift them up and pinch them together to form a parcel. Ⓐ Ⓕ
5. Brush each parcel with beaten egg and, taking care not to brush the cut edges, lay them on a dampened baking sheet. Bake in the preheated oven for 30 minutes until puffed and brown. Serve warm.

Ⓐ May be prepared up to 8 hours in advance. Cover and chill until required.
Ⓕ Uncooked talmouses may be frozen for up to 2 months. Bake from frozen for 35 minutes.

TARTE AU FROMAGE

50 g (2 oz) butter
50 g (2 oz) plain flour
300 ml (½ pint) milk, warmed
225g (8 oz) Lancashire cheese, grated
6 eggs, separated
½ teaspoon salt
½ teaspoon freshly ground black pepper
2 tablespoons snipped fresh chives
1 tablespoon chopped fresh parsley
½ teaspoon Tabasco sauce, or to taste
1 Savoury shortcrust pastry base in a 20 cm (8 inch) deep, loose-bottomed cake tin, baked blind (page 8)
To garnish:
chopped fresh parsley
snipped chives

Preparation time: 30 minutes
Cooking time: 50 minutes
Oven: 200°C, 400°F, Gas Mark 6

This hot soufflé cheesecake is a variation of a classic French supper dish. Serve it with a crisp green salad.

1. Melt the butter in a pan; blend in the flour and cook over a low heat for 2-3 minutes, stirring constantly. Gradually pour on the milk, beating continuously. Draw off the heat and allow to cool slightly.
2. Beat in the grated cheese and the egg yolks, one at a time. Return to a gentle heat and stir until the cheese has melted. Stir in the salt, pepper, chives, parsley and Tabasco. Ⓐ
3. Whip the egg whites until stiff and gently fold into the mixture.
4. Pour the mixture immediately into the pastry case in the cake tin. Bake for 30 minutes until well risen and golden. Carefully slip off the sides of the cake tin, scatter the chopped parsley and chives over and serve immediately.

Ⓐ The sauce may be prepared up to 8 hours in advance. Lay a sheet of buttered paper on top to prevent a skin forming and chill until required.

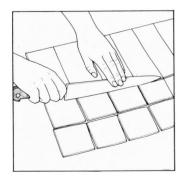

Cutting the puff pastry squares

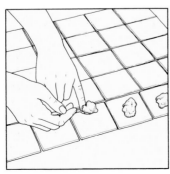

Spooning on the filling

Moistening the edges with water

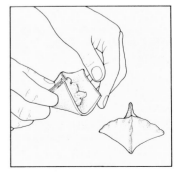

Pinching the edges together

CUCUMBER CHEESECAKE

Serves 8

225 g (8 oz) cucumber, peeled and finely chopped
1 tablespoon salt
3 tablespoons lemon juice
450 g (1 lb) curd cheese
300 ml (½ pint) whipping cream
½ teaspoon salt (optional)
½ teaspoon freshly ground black pepper
1 tablespoon powdered gelatine dissolved in 3 tablespoons
    very hot water
3 tablespoons finely chopped spring onions
2 tablespoons finely chopped fresh coriander or parsley
2 tablespoons finely chopped fresh chives
1 quantity Savoury breadcrumb base (see Avocado and
    prawn cheesecake, page 75)

To garnish:
cucumber slices
fresh chives
fresh coriander or parsley

Preparation time: 25 minutes plus draining and chilling overnight

1. Put the cucumber into a colander and sprinkle the salt and lemon juice over. Stir well then cover with a weighted plate and leave to drain for 1-2 hours. Press out any moisture from the cucumber and pat dry with paper towels.
2. Thoroughly beat the curd cheese. Lightly whip the cream and fold in with the cucumber. Season to taste with salt and pepper if necessary.
3. Stir in the dissolved gelatine and the chopped spring onions, coriander and chives.
4. Turn the mixture into a lightly oiled 1·2 litre (2 pint) fluted brioche mould. Chill for 1-2 hours until set.
5. Press the crumb base on top and chill overnight.
6. When ready to serve, unmould on to a serving plate and garnish with cucumber, chives and fresh coriander.

SMOKED SALMON CHEESE MOULD

Serves 8

3 eggs, separated
300 ml (½ pint) milk
200 g (7 oz) curd cheese
1 teaspoon lemon juice
½ teaspoon freshly ground black pepper
225 g (8 oz) smoked salmon, cut into small dice
3 teaspoons powdered gelatine, dissolved in 3 tablespoons
   very hot water
150 ml (¼ pint) double cream, lightly whipped
1 quantity Savoury breadcrumb base as for Avocado
   and prawn cheesecake (page 75)

To garnish:

8 stuffed olives
fine strips of smoked salmon

Preparation time: 45 minutes plus chilling
Cooking time: 15 minutes

1. Put the egg yolks and the milk in a heatproof bowl over a pan of simmering water and stir until the mixture thickens. Cool.
2. Transfer to a large mixing bowl and beat in the curd cheese, lemon juice and black pepper. Fold in the diced smoked salmon, then mix in the dissolved gelatine and set aside until the mixture is on the point of setting.
3. Whisk the egg whites until stiff and fold them into the mixture. Lightly whip the cream and fold in.
4. Pour into a lightly oiled 1.2 litre (2 pint) fish-shaped mould and chill for 1 hour.
5. Press the savoury breadcrumb base lightly on to the filling in the tin and chill for a further 3-4 hours. Ⓐ
6. To serve, unmould the cheesecake on to a large serving plate and garnish with stuffed olives and strips of salmon.

Ⓐ May be prepared 1 day in advance. Cover, keep chilled and decorate just before serving.

FROM THE LEFT Cucumber cheesecake; Smoked salmon cheese mould

CURD CHEESE AND SPINACH FILO PARCELS

Makes 24
225 g (8 oz) frozen chopped spinach, defrosted and drained
225 g (8 oz) curd cheese
½ teaspoon salt
½ teaspoon freshly ground black pepper
1 egg, well beaten
½ teaspoon grated nutmeg
2 tablespoons pine nuts
225 g (8 oz) filo pastry
120 g (4½ oz) butter, melted

Preparation time: 30 minutes
Cooking time: 10 minutes
Oven: 190°C, 375°F, Gas Mark 5

1. Beat together the spinach, cheese, salt, pepper, egg, nutmeg and pine nuts.
2. Cut a filo sheet into 4 long strips about 7½ cm (3 inches) wide. Brush with melted butter. Place a heaped teaspoonful of filling at the end of one strip and fold the end over it (see pictures on page 9).
3. Fold in the long sides of the pastry then fold over the filled end again and again to produce a squarish parcel. Make 23 more parcels in the same way.
4. Brush each parcel with melted butter and arrange 1 cm (½ inch) apart on greased baking sheets.
5. Bake in the preheated oven for 10 minutes until golden.
6. Serve warm, with drinks or as an hors d'oeuvre.

CHEESE AND SPINACH CORNETS

1 tablespoon butter
2 tablespoons finely chopped shallots
40 g (1½ oz) Parmesam cheese, grated
225 g (8 oz) cooked chopped spinach, drained
100 g (4 oz) ricotta cheese, sieved and drained
pinch of nutmeg
½ teaspoon salt
½ teaspoon freshly ground black pepper
1 egg yolk
12 cooked Savoury pancakes (page 11)

Preparation time: 25 minutes
Cooking time: 10-15 minutes
Oven: 220°C, 425°F, Gas Mark 7

1. Heat the butter in a frying pan and gently fry the shallots until soft and transparent. Set aside.
2. Reserve 1 tablespoon of Parmesan cheese and combine the rest with the spinach and ricotta cheese. Beat in the cooked shallots, nutmeg, salt and pepper. Mix in the egg yolk. **A**
3. To assemble the cornets, fold a pancake in half. Lay 1/12th of the filling in the middle and roll the pancake into a cornet shape. Transfer to a greased baking sheet. Prepare 11 more cornets in the same way. Sprinkle the reserved Parmesan cheese on top.
4. Bake in the preheated oven for 10-15 minutes.
5. Carefully remove from the sheet and serve hot.

A The sauce may be prepared a few hours in advance. Cover and chill until required.

HOT SWISS CHEESE TARTLETS

Makes 24
Savoury shortcrust pastry for 24 tartlet shells (page 8)
120 g (4½ oz) Emmental cheese, grated
65 g (2½ oz) Gruyère cheese, grated
2 eggs, lightly beaten
100 ml (3½ fl oz) milk
100 ml (3½ fl oz) double cream
pinch of nutmeg
½ teaspoon ground white pepper
½ teaspoon salt
To garnish:
cayenne pepper or paprika
24 sprigs fresh parsley

Preparation time: 30 minutes plus chilling
Cooking time: 20 minutes
Oven: 190°C, 375°F, Gas Mark 5

These tartlets are an unusual appetizer to serve with drinks.

1. Roll out the pastry and line 24 greased tartlet shells. Prick the pastry all over with a fork. Chill.
2. Combine the cheeses, and sprinkle half into the lined tartlet shells.
3. Mix the remaining cheese with the beaten eggs, milk, cream, nutmeg, pepper and salt. Blend well.
4. Pour the mixture into the tartlet shells and bake for 20 minutes until risen and brown.
5. Remove from the oven and dust each tart with a little cayenne pepper. Place a sprig of parsley on each tart and serve immediately.

FROM THE LEFT Curd cheese and spinach filo parcels; Cheese and spinach cornets; Hot Swiss cheese tartlets

HERB AND CHEESE STRUDEL

Serves 4-6
25 g (1 oz) butter
2 tablespoons chopped fresh parsley
2 tablespoons chopped chives
1 teaspoon chopped chervil, fresh or dried
2 tablespoons chopped sorrel (optional)
2 tablespoons toasted breadcrumbs
450 g (1 lb) curd cheese
2 egg yolks
150 ml (¼ pint) soured cream
1 teaspoon salt
225 g (8 oz) small French beans, blanched
225 g (8 oz) filo pastry (see opposite)
120 g (4½ oz) unsalted butter, melted

Preparation time: 45 minutes
Cooking time: 40 minutes
Oven: 200°C, 400°F, Gas Mark 6

1. Melt the butter in a pan and gently fry the herbs and breadcrumbs for 2 minutes. Allow to cool.
2. Beat together the cheese, yolks, soured cream and salt, then stir in the cooled herb and crumb mixture.
3. Prepare the filo pastry in buttered layers on a clean tea towel as for Strudel cheese roll (page 37), finishing with a coating of melted butter.
4. Spread the filling over the pastry to within 2.5 cm (1 inch) of the edges. Distribute the beans, widthways, over the length of the filling.
5. Fold in the ends of the pastry and, using the tea towel as an aid, carefully roll up the strudel from the short side.
6. Use the tea towel to transfer the strudel to a greased baking sheet, seam side down, and brush the strudel with melted butter. Bake in the preheated oven for 40 minutes until golden.
7. Serve hot.

TO USE FILO PASTRY

Filo pastry can be bought ready-made from Greek and Middle Eastern stores and good delicatessens. When using filo you must work quickly as it dries out and becomes brittle once it is exposed to the air. Filo will keep for up to 2 months in the freezer.

For each 450 g (1 lb) packet of filo pastry, you will need 225 g (8 oz) melted unsalted butter. Lay a clean tea towel on a work top and dust with flour. Unwrap the dough and remove half. Cover the rest until it is needed to prevent it drying out. Peel off 1 sheet of filo, lay it on the cloth and brush all over with melted butter. Lay another sheet on top and brush with butter. Continue until all the pastry has been used. Fill according to recipe instructions.

FROM THE LEFT Herb and cheese strudel; Curried seafood and cheese pancakes

CURRIED SEAFOOD AND CHEESE PANCAKES

Serves 6
12 Savoury pancakes (page 11)
Fish filling:
4 tablespoons olive oil
225 g (8 oz) prawns, cooked and peeled
225 g (8 oz) firm fish, cooked and flaked
1 tablespoon finely chopped fresh parsley
1 teaspoon curry powder
½ teaspoon Tabasco sauce
1 tablespoon tomato purée
1 × 225 g (8 oz) can tomatoes, drained
1 teaspoon salt
½ teaspoon freshly ground black pepper
Cheese filling:
300 g (11 oz) curd cheese
3 eggs, separated
½ teaspoon freshly ground black pepper
To garnish:
2 tablespoons grated Parmesan cheese
cooked peeled prawns
sprigs of fresh parsley

Preparation time: 25 minutes plus setting
Cooking time: 10-15 minutes
Oven: 220°C, 425°F, Gas Mark 7

Many types of fish can be used for this pie; turbot, haddock, hake and salmon are all good. Choose according to seasonal availability.

1. To make the fish filling, heat the oil in a pan and fry the prawns and fish for 2 minutes over a medium heat.
2. Stir in the parsley, curry powder, Tabasco, tomato purée and tomatoes; cook gently for 15 minutes. Season with salt and black pepper and set aside. **A**
3. To make the cheese filling, beat together the curd cheese, egg yolks and pepper. Whisk the egg whites until stiff and fold them in.
4. To assemble the pancakes, spoon 1/12th of the fish filling on to a pancake, just off centre. Spoon 1/12th of the cheese filling next to it and roll up. Transfer to a greased baking tray. Fill the remaining pancakes in the same way.
5. Dust the tops with the Parmesan cheese and bake in the preheated oven for 10-15 minutes.
6. To serve, carefully remove the pancakes and garnish with parsley and prawns.

A The fish sauce may be prepared 8 hours in advance. Cover and chill until required.

CHEESE SOUFFLÉ ROLLS

Serves 4-6
Soufflé base:
120 g (4½ oz) butter
90 g (3½ oz) flour
685 ml (1 pint 3 fl oz) milk
½ teaspoon salt
freshly ground black pepper
8 eggs, separated
100 g (4 oz) Cheddar cheese, grated
Filling:
1 tablespoon butter
2 tablespoons finely chopped shallots
175 g (6 oz) mushrooms, finely chopped
100 g (4 oz) Parma or other ham, finely chopped
225 g (8 oz) cooked chopped spinach, well drained
100 g (4 oz) mozzarella or gruyère cheese, grated
pinch of nutmeg
½ teaspoon salt
pinch of black pepper

Preparation time: 45 minutes
Cooking time: 50 minutes
Oven: 200°C, 400°F, Gas Mark 6

Serve the rolls for lunch or supper with a crisp green salad. To serve 3-4, simply use half quantities and fill only 1 baking tray.

1. Line 2 rectangular Swiss roll tins 25 × 36 cm (10 × 14 inches) with non-stick silicone paper.
2. Melt the butter in a pan, blend in the flour and cook over a low heat for 2-3 minutes, stirring constantly. Gradually pour on the milk, beating continuously. Simmer the mixture gently, stirring, for 5 minutes then season with salt and pepper. Pour off half and reserve.
3. Add the egg yolks, one by one, to the remaining sauce and then beat in the cheese. Stir over a gentle heat for 2-3 minutes until well combined.
4. Whip up the egg whites until stiff and gently fold into the cheese sauce.
5. Divide the mixture between the lined tins, smoothing it well into the corners. Bake for 15 minutes.
6. Meanwhile make the filling. Melt the butter in a large frying pan and gently fry the shallots, mushrooms and ham for 5 minutes. Add the spinach, the reserved sauce and cheese, nutmeg, salt and pepper.
7. When the soufflés are well risen and lightly browned remove from the oven and immediately turn them out on to clean sheets of silicone paper. Peel off the lining papers.
8. Divide the warm filling over the 2 bases, spreading it to within 1 cm (½ inch) of the edges. Roll up each soufflé base from the short side.
9. If not being served immediately, the soufflé rolls may be kept warm in the switched off oven for up to 15 minutes.

AVOCADO AND PRAWN CHEESECAKE

Serves 12
6 teaspoons powdered gelatine
300 ml (½ pint) hot chicken stock
2 large avocados
1 tablespoon chopped spring onion
½ teaspoon salt
½ teaspoon freshly ground white pepper
2 teaspoons Worcestershire sauce
½-1 teaspoon Tabasco sauce
150 ml (¼ pint) double cream, whipped
150 g (5 oz) curd cheese
2 egg whites
250 g (9 oz) peeled prawns
few sprigs curly endive, to garnish
Savoury breadcrumb base:
75 g (3 oz) toasted breadcrumbs
75 g (3 oz) butter, melted
1 tablespoon chopped fresh parsley
pinch of nutmeg

Preparation time: 45 minutes plus chilling

1. Dissolve the gelatine in 4 tablespoons of hot stock (page 16).
2. Peel and mash the avocados. Mix the rest of the stock with the mashed avocados, chopped spring onion, salt, pepper, Worcestershire and Tabasco sauces. Blend well.
3. Mix in the dissolved gelatine and beat until smooth. Put the mixture to one side until on the point of setting.
4. Whip the double cream until stiff and fold into the curd cheese; then fold both into the stiffened avocado mixture. Beat the egg whites until stiff and fold in.
5. Pour the mixture into a lightly oiled 24 cm (9½ inch) ring mould. Cover with cling film and chill overnight.
6. Make the breadcrumb base as for the basic recipe on page 7 and lightly press it on to the chilled filling in the mould. Chill for one hour more. Ⓐ
7. To serve, unmould the cheesecake on to a large serving dish. Fill the centre with curly endive and arrange the prawns on top.

Ⓐ May be prepared 1 day in advance. Cover and chill until required.

FROM THE LEFT Cheese soufflé roll; Avocado and prawn cheesecake

COTTAGE CHEESE KONAFA

Serves 8-10
450 g (1 lb) konafa pastry
225 g (8 oz) unsalted butter, melted
450 g (1 lb) cottage cheese, sieved, or curd cheese
100 g (4 oz) Cheddar cheese, grated
3 eggs, lightly beaten
1 tablespoon dried mint
½ teaspoon ground nutmeg
½ teaspoon freshly ground black pepper

Preparation time: 30 minutes
Cooking time: 1 hour
Oven: 180°C, 350°F, Gas Mark 4
then: 230°C, 450°F, Gas Mark 8

This is a Middle Eastern savoury cheesecake which can be served as a starter or as a light supper dish. Konafa pastry looks like soft white strands of uncooked vermicelli and can be bought in Greek and Middle Eastern shops.

1. Place the konafa pastry in a large bowl and gently pull the strands apart. Pour over the melted butter and toss lightly until each strand is coated.
2. Grease a 23 cm (9 inch) springform tin and firmly press in half the pastry.
3. Make the filling by beating together the curd cheese, grated cheese, beaten eggs, mint, nutmeg and black pepper.
4. Spoon the filling in to the tin. Lay the rest of the pastry on top and press it down firmly. Ⓐ
5. Bake in the preheated oven for 35 minutes, then increase the temperature and bake for a further 15 minutes.
6. Carefully remove the sides of the tin. Serve hot cut in wedges.

Ⓐ The uncooked konafa may be prepared 1-2 hours in advance. Cover and keep chilled.

CHEESE AND AUBERGINE FLAN

Serves 6
750 g (1¾ lb) aubergines, cut into 6 mm (¼ inch) slices
2½ tablespoons salt
2 tablespoons olive oil
375 g (13 oz) curd cheese
3 eggs
2 tablespoons fresh dill, chopped, or 1 teaspoon dried dill
2 tablespoons fresh basil, chopped, or 1 tablespoon dried basil
½ teaspoon freshly ground black pepper
Savoury shortcrust pastry case in a 22 cm (8½ inch) springform tin, baked blind (page 8)
1 egg white, lightly beaten
2 tablespoons grated Parmesan cheese
sprigs of fresh dill and basil, to garnish

Preparation time: 30 minutes plus draining
Cooking time: 1 hour 10 minutes
Oven: 180°C, 350°F, Gas Mark 4

1. Lay the aubergines in a colander and sprinkle with the salt. Stir well and leave to drain for 30 minutes. Rinse, squeeze out the water and dry with paper towels.
2. Brush the slices lightly with oil and grill for 5 minutes on each side to soften.
3. Blend together the curd cheese, eggs, dill and basil. Season to taste with salt and pepper.
4. Brush the base of the pastry with beaten egg white.
5. Arrange half the aubergine slices in the bottom of the case, cover with the filling, and lay the rest of the aubergine slices on top. Scatter the Parmesan over.
6. Bake in a preheated oven for 1 hour. Ⓐ Ⓕ
7. Serve hot, garnished with sprigs of dill and basil and with a crisp green salad.

Ⓐ May be cooked up to 8 hours in advance. Cover with tin foil and reheat when required.
Ⓕ May be frozen for 2 months. Reheat from frozen for about 40 minutes at 160°C, 325°F, Gas Mark 3.

Gently pull apart the strands of konafa pastry

Firmly press half the konafa pastry into the springform tin

Spoon the filling into the tin, on top of the pastry

Lay the remaining pastry on top then press it down firmly

FROM THE LEFT Cottage cheese konafa; Cheese and aubergine flan

MEDITERRANEAN CHEESE FILO

Serves 4-6

50 g (2 oz) butter
50 g (2 oz) onion, finely chopped
2 tablespoons toasted breadcrumbs
4 tablespoons chopped fresh coriander
2 tablespoons grated lemon zest
1 egg
450 g (1 lb) curd cheese
1 teaspoon salt
225 g (½ lb) filo pastry (see page 73)
120 g (4½ oz) unsalted butter, melted

Preparation time: 20-25 minutes
Cooking time: 40 minutes
Oven: 200°C, 400°F, Gas Mark 6

1. Melt the butter in a pan and gently fry the onion until transparent.
2. Stir in the breadcrumbs, coriander and lemon zest and fry lightly. Set aside.
3. Combine the egg with the curd cheese and salt. Stir in the onion and herb mixture.
4. Prepare the filo pastry in buttered layers on a clean tea towel as for Strudel cheese roll (page 37), finishing with a coating of butter.
5. Spread the filling over the pastry to within 2.5 cm (1 inch) of the edges. Fold over the ends of the pastry and carefully roll up the pastry from the short side.
6. Transfer to a greased baking sheet, seam side down, and brush with melted butter.
7. Bake in the preheated oven for 40 minutes until puffed and golden.
8. Serve hot.

MUSHROOM AND PARSLEY PIZZA CHEESECAKES

Serves 4

175 g (6 oz) Cheddar cheese, grated
1 tablespoon plain flour
pinch of salt
1 teaspoon freshly ground black pepper
2 eggs
1 tablespoon Kirsch
15 g (½ oz) butter
40 g (1½ oz) chopped onion
1 × 225 g (8 oz) can tomatoes, drained, seeded and chopped
100 g (4 oz) mushrooms, sliced
100 g (4 oz) cooked ham, chopped
1½ tablespoons chopped fresh parsley or coriander
1 quantity Pizza dough (see opposite)

Preparation time: 30 minutes
Cooking time: 35 minutes
Oven: 220°C, 425°F, Gas Mark 7

1. Mix together the Cheddar cheese, flour, salt and pepper. Beat in the eggs, one at a time, stir in the Kirsch and chill for 10 minutes to thicken.

2. Heat the butter in a frying pan and gently cook the onion for 2 minutes to soften. Stir into the cheese mixture with the tomatoes, mushrooms, ham and parsley or coriander. **A**

3. Divide the pizza dough in four. Roll out each piece into a 15 cm (6 inch) circle and spread the filling thickly on the dough circles. **F** Set them on lightly greased baking trays and bake in a preheated oven for 35 minutes.

4. Serve hot, with a salad as a light lunch, or cut into wedges with aperitifs.

A The filling may be made 2-3 hours in advance. Cover and chill until required.

F The uncooked pizza cakes may be frozen for up to 1 month. Defrost at room temperature for 1 hour.

MOZZARELLA AND TOMATO TART

Serves 4

150 g (5 oz) puff pastry or Savoury shortcrust pastry for a
    20 cm (8 inch) springform tin (page 8)
350 g (12 oz) large Mediterranean tomatoes, cut into 1 cm
    (½ inch) slices, pips removed
2½ tablespoons olive oil
½ teaspoon salt
½ teaspoon freshly ground black pepper
1 tablespoon herb mustard
200 g (7 oz) mozzarella cheese, cut into 6 mm (¼ inch)
    slices
2 tablespoons chopped fresh coriander or 1 tablespoon
    powdered coriander
sprigs of fresh coriander, to garnish

Preparation time: 25 minutes plus marinating
Cooking time: 40-50 minutes
Oven: 190°C, 375°F, Gas Mark 5

Olive oil, tomatoes and fresh coriander give this recipe
a marked Provençal flavour. Serve the tart as a tasty
summer supper dish.

1. Grease a 20 cm (8 inch) springform tin. Line with
pastry so that the pastry extends over the base and
halfway up the sides. Prick all over with a fork. Chill.
2. Meanwhile lay the tomato slices on a large plate and
brush them with olive oil. Sprinkle with the salt and
pepper and leave to marinate for 15 minutes, turning
occasionally.
3. Spread the mustard over the chilled pastry base,
then arrange the mozzarella slices on top, scattering
over a little of the coriander as you go. Lay the
marinated tomato slices on top and sprinkle with any
marinade juices left over.
4. Sprinkle the rest of the coriander over and bake in a
preheated oven for 40-50 minutes. Cool on a wire tray
for 15 minutes.
5. Carefully remove the sides of the tin and serve
lukewarm, garnished with coriander sprigs.

PIZZA DOUGH

225 g (8 oz) self-raising flour
1 teaspoon baking powder
½ teaspoon salt
25 g (1 oz) butter
50 g (2 oz) Cheddar cheese, grated
150 ml (¼ pint) milk

Preparation time: 15 minutes

This dough does not keep well, and should be made
just before it is used.

1. Sift the flour with the baking powder and salt into a
bowl.
2. Rub in the butter, then mix in the cheese.
3. Stir in the milk and blend to a rough dough.
4. Knead on a floured work top for 2-3 minutes until
smooth.
5. Wrap and leave to rest whilst making the filling.

Variation:
For Italian-style pizza cheesecakes substitute mozzarella cheese for the Cheddar, 6 chopped anchovy fillets
for the ham and 2 teaspoons oregano for the parsley or
coriander. Proceed as above, omitting the salt.

FROM THE LEFT Mushroom and parsley pizza cheesecakes with Italian-style pizza
cheesecakes variation; Mozzarella and tomato tart

INDEX